P9-ARD-571

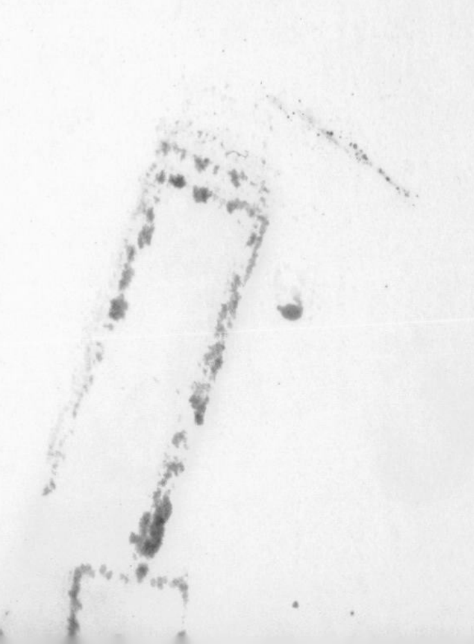

LEGACY OF LOVE

OTHER BOOKS BY JULIA DAVIS

NOVELS

The Sun Climbs Slow
Cloud on the Land
Bridle the Wind
Eagle on the Sun

HISTORY

The Shenandoah (Rivers of America)

CHILDREN'S BOOKS

Swords of the Vikings
Vaino, a Boy of Finland
Mountains Are Free
Stonewall Jackson
Remember and Forget
Peter Hale
No Other White Men

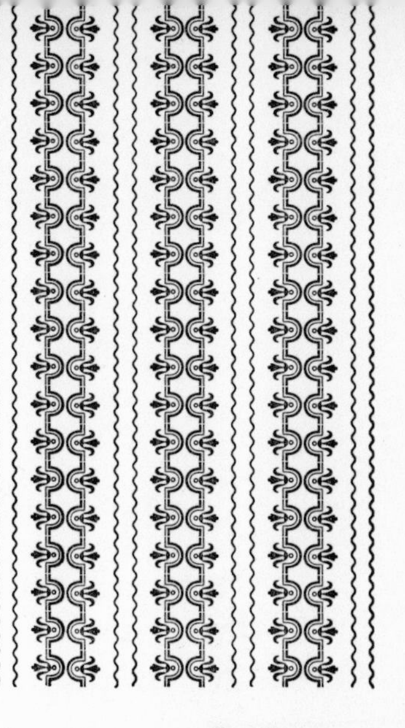

JULIA DAVIS *Legacy of Love*

HARCOURT, BRACE & WORLD, INC.

NEW YORK

First edition.
Library of Congress
Catalog Card Number: 61-11914
Printed in the
United States of America

FOR ANNE AND LOUISE

AND THE NEW TWIGS

Epilogue to Yesterday

Sometimes there comes a pause in life when the familiar forward motion no longer serves, when new direction must be sought. In such a pause I came into possession of chests and boxes of old papers, letters, scrapbooks, diaries. By the open fire at Media I read them.

I went back then to my roots. The older generations came again to life, this time in the round, not merely as seen by the young. Reading, I recalled my family in every sense of that good word, and found my signposts for the future.

These were not all successful people in a worldly way, but each was valiant. Their story cannot be a connected narrative; it is a tapestry of memories.

When I was born my mother died. Four grandparents, ten aunts, ten uncles, a father, a stepmother, and two firm first cousins brought up the child. Threading my early path among them I learned to get on with almost anyone—an aptitude that has made trouble for me ever since. It is still hard for me to believe that the lamb will not lie down with the lion, given a chance to see what a lovable lion it is.

I remember a tall old house where life moved as quietly as a brain wave, where every member of the family had a separate room for reading or study and was expected to use it. Fourteen-foot ceilings lofted above; the long front hall gloomed like a cave. Heavy lace curtains and shades darkened parlors, and in the library a bookcase blocked the bay window. On the thick carpets footsteps made no sound. The silence rang in my ears.

I remember a wide farm run over by generations of children; a family in which I was the twelfth child, but not the last; an open sunny house with seven outside doors, never locked; and a grove of oaks more important to daily living than the house itself. The oaks were our home.

One way of life developed a group of unrepentant individualists, the other a family that quite properly called itself a clan. Then, with the years, my father, moving successfully forward, carried me with him.

The life of the mind, the life of the heart, the life of the great world. It has not been easy or, indeed, always possible to combine the three. Yet the first and second feed each other and point the way to survival in the third.

Of my father I shall tell only the family side. It is better for someone else to write of his public life. Of his career in politics, his Presidential campaign, his service as ambassador, his legal successes, I can only put up markers for the interested. If there is here recorded more than his reticent spirit would have permitted, it is because, looking into his heart, I have loved what I saw there. I weep for sorrows that grieve him no longer and find it faithful to his memory to recount them.

Through my grandparents I shared three generations of experience, a span of more than a century. That world differed from ours, at least outwardly; it must be pictured in order to make them clear. In their own day they adapted to changing times. If they were living now they could adapt. They reacted to suffering with a determination to fight it—possibly with a regrettable display of temper. They were ambitious to improve themselves, but more inwardly than outwardly. They were independent to a fault. And they loved work.

Diverse to exaggeration, all of them had four traits in common: a deep faith in their country, for which they were prepared to sacrifice; a willingness to face whatever fate brought; a habit of consulting their own consciences before they consulted anything else; and, above all, the power to love.

Let me then speak for them, forward in time, and, hopefully, let me do them justice.

JULIA DAVIS

Media
1960

PART ONE

I

Two months after he graduated from Washington and Lee, young John Davis went to tutor the children of a Major McDonald (once of J. E. B. Stuart's cavalry), who lived on a farm in the Shenandoah Valley near Charles Town. The job paid only three hundred dollars a year with room and board, but John needed time to make up his mind what lifework to follow, so he accepted it. It proved to be an appointment with fate.

The train from his home in Clarksburg, in central West Virginia, stopped in the gray dawn at the crossing called Shenandoah Junction and he climbed down. The station at the Junction was never crowded. So early only one man waited there, the Major. As they drove off together in the dayton behind old Bob, John took a cautious look at his employer. A short, wiry man, the Major wore a closely cropped white beard to hide the scar made by a bullet at Appomattox. His speech was hurried and indistinct, his movements hasty, his manner brisk and imperious. He must have a temper, John thought, and hoped to please. John J. Davis, John's father, had made inquiries and found the Mc-

Donalds a highly respected and Christian family. John must do his best.

The Major greeted him cordially as one man to another, and the talk turned to politics, as most talk between men did in West Virginia.

"How do you expect to vote in November, Mr. Davis?"

"I have not planned to go home for the elections, Major."

(It would never do to admit that he would not be twenty-one years old until April.)

The road wound through a lovely, gently rolling countryside, rolling gently to the wall of the Blue Ridge Mountains, which on that morning deserved their name. The Major observed his young man. Tall, so thin that his college nickname had been Bones, with dark hair, sky-blue eyes, a shy smile, and a jimber jaw, he did not look strong, but he had been highly recommended. Major McDonald had foreseen difficulties in educating his children when he moved them from Louisville to the farm, for schools were poor in Charles Town, and winter roads slushy or impassable. Tutoring seemed the solution, and among several candidates John Davis had been selected, sight unseen. The Major was not a man to waver in his decisions. John Davis would have to do.

He explained that there would be fifteen pupils, "nine in our house, and six of my wife's nieces and nephews from the adjoining place. My boy Eddie is grown and going into law in Louisville."

While John was digesting this they turned into the lane through the oak woods at Media, and within minutes he met more people gathered around the breakfast table than he had ever seen in one family.

Next day he wrote his mother of dizzying efforts to arrange a schedule and a curriculum and to find out what, "if anything," had already been learned. The young lady daughters, Anne and

Julia, were to be improved by the study of botany and French. Three broad adolescents, Will, Peerce, and Angus, each of whom looked, and was, strong enough to throw a steer, must be prepared for college. Dark little Mary and golden little Marshall were to be guided through the early grades, while the six-year-olds, John and Lill, learned to read and write. The cousins must be fitted in with their contemporaries. All this, simultaneously, in a one-room log cabin behind the house.

John reported that the Major was a man one could respect and that Mrs. McDonald was gentle and sweet. "Miss Julia, who is about eighteen, would be pretty if it were not for a scar on her cheek caused by falling into a fireplace when she was a child. I think you may tell Nan (his sister who had teased him about courting the unmarried daughters) Miss Julia is the one." His premonition proved correct.

He was quartered in the "boys' rooms," the old stone back of the house reached by an outside staircase, which discouraged loitering in winter. The little round wood stove went out at night, and in the morning when they washed, if they washed, they broke the ice in their pitchers. It was a cold trip to the three-holer under the trumpet vine. The Major did not believe in pampering his sons.

His discipline required that they behave in the schoolroom, but outside of it the new teacher was fair game. John gave up wearing a hat—too fine a target for snowballs. No marksman, he was chivvied into shooting at a squirrel, hit it by luck, and had the good sense not to shoot again during his stay. Above all else, his contemplative nature missed quiet and privacy. If he stayed in his room to read, the family thought him lonely and sought him out. If he went for a walk, one of the children kept him company. He escaped by assigning himself the daily chore of walking across the fields to pick up the mail at the Junction, two miles away.

The life was considerably more rugged than anything to which he had been accustomed, the shabby old house pretended to nothing, yet he found himself growing to like it. It stood in a grove of magnificent oaks and looked out broadly across the chequered fields and green pastures of the Shenandoah Valley to the ever-changing mountains.

Thanks to the War, the McDonalds had no money for improvements. With no water except what was drawn from outside cisterns, no heat except from stoves or open fires, no light except for oil lamps, Media still possessed something intangible yet plain to all who came there; something which drew the visitors back again and again. It was infused with love.

The source and fountainhead of all this joy were the explosive Major and his gentle wife. They set the pattern for their home, and although by modern standards they did not have "a moment to themselves," they lived as they wished to live.

When John Davis first met the family, they themselves were getting used to country life. They had grown up in Louisville, spending only summer vacations on the farm which their mother had inherited from her grandfather. The Major's health failed at sixty, and the doctor ordered him to give up the practice of law. He turned himself into a farmer for another active twenty years.

The younger children adapted, but the two older girls missed their city friends. Anne, pretty, ambitious, talented—and deaf—confined to one trip to town a week behind a poky horse, felt buried alive and said so. Julia, who lived in the happiness of others, took over the chores which her mother did not have time to do.

She was small, and full of what the Major called "chirping spirits." Because of her singing he nicknamed her Birdie. Her copper-brown hair waved charmingly no matter how hastily she did it up, and her eyes were the McDonald smoky blue. The younger members of the family swarmed about her. "We all love Jule," said Angus.

Before long she could not help noticing that the young tutor followed her around at her daily tasks, feeding the chickens, digging in the garden, turning the churn. She wore the keys to the household stores at her belt and dealt out the whisky for special occasions. John Davis called her Hebe.

"You are such an absurd man," she said. "I told you I adore funny people. I expect to get *fat* laughing at your nonsense some day."

The six little brothers and sisters saw no reason to give them time for courting. "It was an uphill business with you, darling," John wrote her, "until that botany helped us out." Even then eleven-year-old Mary tagged along and had to be sent to far corners of the fields for specimens.

They could not become engaged. John Davis did not yet know what he was going to do in life, except that he would not remain a tutor on a salary of three hundred a year. They could only become engaged to be engaged, and meet shrewd guessing by stouthearted denials.

When writing of my fathers and mothers, how shall I write of my mother, whom I never knew? She was a fragrance, an atmosphere in my childish life. Grandmother Davis spoke of her often, "your dear Mother," invisible but present, a privately owned guardian angel. Grandmother McDonald spoke of her never. She was a tear in the Major's eye, the flowers from home that we laid in the churchyard every Sunday as we went to church, a tender smile of recollection on the faces of my uncles and aunts. My father could not trust himself to mention her.

I was twenty and in England when he asked my stepmother to give me her engagement ring, which had been put away for me. He saw it on my finger as we clacked cheerfully through the countryside on an English train, he riding backwards as was his unselfish wont. His face flushed violently, his eyes filled, he buried himself in the paper which he had finished reading. I never again wore the ring where he could see it.

After his death I found her letters, tied with utilitarian string, unromantically preserved in an old laundry case lodged in the attic of his home on Long Island. They had traveled a long way.

From the yellowed pages, covered with her graceful script, as steady as her heart, a personality emerges. Hers was a brief, sweet, evanescent story.

Tutoring ended, promises secretly made, John Davis went back across the Alleghenies to Clarksburg to clerk in his father's office and find out whether he really liked the law. He did. Borrowing from his father, he returned to Washington and Lee for the only year of law school he ever had, and took his degree. Licenses in those days were issued by a judge.

"What do you want me to say, John?" the judge asked.

John wrote out a testimonial of his competence in his own hand, and the judge signed it.

That autumn Washington and Lee surprised him by the offer of an instructorship in their law school. He took it and by his own report learned more law than he had ever done in the same length of time, all at the expense of his pupils.

Somewhere along the way he and Julia, too young for the strain of waiting, fell out. They still wrote occasionally, merely as friends. "Certain of my dreams have proved themselves phantoms," John hinted. When the university asked him to stay on, it seemed natural to inquire of Julia, quite impersonally, whether she thought the life of a professor or that of a lawyer more desirable.

She told him, as she always did, to follow his own preferences. Active practice won out, as it always would, and on his way home John rode his bicycle, his "wheel," up the Valley to spend a night at Media. It was a casual visit, a brief call on a family which had been kind to him, a stop which it would have been rude not to make. He took lifelong pride in behaving reasonably rather than emotionally.

The oaks still stood. The merry family still gathered around the mahogany table. Miss Julia was still there, and still Miss Julia. He fetched up the courage to get her off by herself, and she confessed that he still had her heart. The sun went back into place.

From Clarksburg he wrote her: "I am deeply glad that I went to Media, happier dearest than I have been for a long time. I am a one woman man now henceforth, as I have been in my heart since I first knew you, and I am thankful it is so. I was badgering Mother last night about any one of a number of girls who might become her daughter-in-law; after several pious 'God forbids' she finally wound up, 'I like Julia McDonald. She is my preference over all of them.' I shall only add that in my heart I echo her words."

"I'm taken up and done for," John admitted. Now his problem was to earn enough money for "lawful awful wedlock."

"I told Father I was going to insert my card (professional term for ad) in the newspaper. 'Wait a minute and I'll write it for you.' I waited, and he wrote on the machine:

JOHN J. DAVIS JOHN W. DAVIS
DAVIS AND DAVIS
ATTORNEYS AT LAW
CLARKSBURG, W. VA.

"I was surprised and greatly pleased, because I thought that if he ever did couple my name with his as a partner, it would be only after he had tried and tested me."

Julia's stout loyalty and common sense could not allow anyone to be too modest about her John, even the man himself.

"Your father is as proud of that as you are."

The practice did not flood in. The first case concerned a strayed turkey hen and her twenty-nine chicks. "This do be a proud day indade—but I'll have to argue it, and I'd about as soon perish miserably."

He lost the case, and that night in the depths of gloom he told his father that he did not think he would ever make a lawyer. John J. Davis, a genuinely eloquent man, gave him a thorough tongue lashing for poltroonery. He crept upstairs abashed, determined to do better, and also determined not to confide any more doubts to his father. After all, he had Julia to confide in. "Not much ice between us now, eh, sweetheart?"

"I never go into a trial without being more or less frightened and anxious to quit the field. I don't believe the ice will ever be broken for me, for I dread a trial now as much as when I first began to practice. I've been regretting I did not speak in the ejectant case, as I don't believe I ought to miss any chance to practice my feeble oratorical powers when the results would not be too disastrous to the unfortunate client. There are times when I wonder if I will ever make a lawyer, but if I fail it will not be, I can honestly say, from want of labor."

He wrote daily, late at night in his little office, when the last dusty law book had been returned to its shelf, or the last word of a brief pecked out on the typewriter. He wrote between clients, or beside the gas fire in the silence of the high gloomy house which his father had built. Like most truly reticent people, when he once lowered his defenses he let them down completely, turning his heart inside out for his Julia—self doubts, depressions, moments of elation, everything.

"I am as awkward in a parlor as a rheumatic hippopotamus. You'll have to try to make something of me, but you have a hard stick to whittle."

"My trouble is not lack of work, but that the fees are small and hard to get. People seem to think that lawyers belong to another race and can wait indefinitely for their pay. It's hard to be content when I am poorer than I was six months ago, and yet have happiness supreme in reach if but the cash were here. It must be my fault. Other men make money. I would mind less if I tried less, but I know I have hit about my best lick."

When he made a mistake in a case he berated himself, "as poor a lawyer as ever imposed his sheepskin on a long-suffering public."

Occasionally an upswing caught him, as if by surprise. "I have been so fortunate in my life so far that I shudder to think of the amount of misery I shall have to endure to square things up. Of all the blessings Providence has given me, the greatest is the love of Julia McDonald."

Her sunny, steady, extroverted disposition gave him exactly what he needed. Out of a busy family life, so distracting that she could not brood over their separation, she sent him daily encouragement. She wrote him from the schoolroom, "my Parnassus," where she taught the younger children. "There's no news, so you will have to hear the old old story. While Lill and John, my old standbys, are struggling with decimal fractions, I am laying up a supply of love that will last for life, and help me to be all I want to be for you."

She wrote while Mary practiced, while Cousin Net told jokes. "I love you even if I haven't time to get romantic. Marshall wanted to learn Latin so I volunteered to help him every evening, although I knew my writing time would suffer." She wrote him after sitting up late to play chess with Percy, who seemed to need cheering, after going to town to straighten out the books in the store which Will briefly and unsuccessfully kept, after reading *Scottish Chiefs* to John and Lill, during which both she and John wept so much that she had to let Lill do the reading. "Lill said she would have cried, if we had not done so much of it."

Always she knew how to hearten him. He was not to worry. She would rather be loved and respected than have ten thousand dollars. ("Your price is low enough," said John.) It was up to a girl to decide whether or not she wished to engage herself to a man and wait for him. She much preferred to know that he loved her when she was so much in love with him.

"Someday John W. Davis's name will be heard far and wide, and won't I be happy and proud to own you when that day comes? My dear old fellow, you are anything but commonplace. You are a brilliant exception to the rule of young barristers. All I want in my house is the man I love. After that I don't care if we have but one chair. You can use it and I will sit on the windowsill. I have heard of a couple who live on seven hundred a year."

John had the answer for that. "I wouldn't attempt it, out of consideration for you and my creditors."

"All right," Julia told him. "If you dread the effects of poverty on your temper, and that it will keep you from being pleasant around home, why you're a man and will have to get over it."

Then Washington and Lee surprisingly offered John a full professorship, with a salary of two thousand a year. He asked Julia's advice. He always enjoyed asking advice and then doing as he pleased. Should he take this security, enough to marry on, or should he continue to battle his way at the bar, declining as more than his due the half of the proceeds which his father generously offered him, and filled with honest doubt as to whether the practice could ever support two families?

Julia understood her man. She wrote that she would be happy in any path he chose. She would marry, or would wait. She had complete faith in the outcome.

He declined the professorship. It was secure, but it was limited. His father needed him. All this was true, but it was also true that he had fallen in love with the law. After a few regretful backward looks, he worked with renewed energy. "Loafing wears out sooner than work does." On some mornings he reached his office at six thirty, and came home for a hasty breakfast at eight. Midnight often struck before he finished his working day.

"Although I have been worried and pulled first this way and that until I am dead tired, I wouldn't give one day like this for a dozen droned away in a classroom. I would have eaten my heart out if I had been in Lexington this winter, with all this going on here."

His letters began to sound a note which was to become the dominating theme of his life. "You have but one rival in my affections, dear. I love my work."

By February 1898 he felt far enough along to come to Media and "speak my piece to the Major." Although he had given Julia a diamond ring at Christmas, which she wore, the formality of asking for a daughter's hand was not one which the Major would be likely to waive. Julia declined the opportunity to be present at the interview. "Don't you dare to put your awful question to Papa before me." John ventured to hope that there would be no disposition to resist the inevitable. The Major could not have been completely surprised, and apparently he took it well.

The outbreak of the Spanish American War threw a shadow over the young couple. Would John have to go? Would the boys? Percy and Angus, by then at West Virginia University, tried to volunteer in true McDonald style. Their father hurried out to see them and persuaded them to finish their term.

"I believe that history will recognize the war as a mistake," John wrote. "It may revive business, but it will increase the national debt, and change the country from a home-keeping and peaceful nation into a colonial and military one." He decided to wait until he was called. "The whole idea of a war for humanitarian reasons is absurd on the face of it."

He and Julia lived under another shadow, but, wrapped in their dream, they did not recognize it as serious. She fell ill. "I think I took a little cold in my journeys to and from the slaughterhouse. How unpoetic and unromantic to put that in a love letter!"

She was a small woman, not strong, but with the heart to work like a man if by so doing she could help those she loved. She lifted washtubs full of sausage, ran on her feet all day, then had extreme pains and lost consciousness, once for almost half an hour. The doctor put her to bed, an operation threatened, a visiting cousin was shocked by her appearance.

John fumed at not being given a precise diagnosis. "I don't know from all this roundabout talk whether you are on the verge of *eclampus vitus* or *aurora borealis*. Placed, as I suppose I must be, at the mercy of the conventionalities, I can do nothing but fret away until I know you are quite well."

When Julia, always obedient to his wishes, wrote him a letter which he must *burn* as soon as he had read it, he was touched by this evidence of their oneness, and glad she was not a prude.

She did not recover easily. She visited in Richmond and could not get out of the house for two weeks, rested at Rockledge Springs with her mother, was taken to Nantucket by Cousin Net, where she acquired a new beau to whom she had to explain that her heart was not free. Whenever she rested she felt better, "as impident as a fly." ("I am glad to hear my bird singing again," the Major said.) Whenever she felt better she went back to work and to lacing her eighteen-inch waist by tying the corset strings to the bedpost. (John thought she had one of the prettiest figures he had ever seen.)

Even the cold winter in the draughty house could not dull

her spirits. "Everything is cold and stiff except the genial humor of the family. We never lack for sunshine indoors."

She could be happy too in the progress made by her diligent young man. His cases increased in interest. He learned, and never forgot, how to use in argument only fifty minutes of his allotted hour and a half. He fumed over the opinions of an inadequate judge. "I can understand inelegance of diction, but I cannot see how anyone can write so that no one can understand what he is driving at." He almost broke a thumb hitting another attorney in the courtroom, and his fine was remitted because the "personal encounter" was a just defense of his father. "I would not have cared if the fine had stayed. I got my money's worth, because mine were the only licks that landed."

Under pressure of work, Davis and Davis took the unprecedented step of hiring a stenographer, and what a help it was to have her! "Someday I hope there will be a letup in this terrible drive." (There never was; at eighty-two he was still joyously, complainingly at it.)

"One must love the law to be great in it, but I suppose that is true of all professions."

Although brilliant in the courtroom, John J. Davis did not make an easy partner. Young John loved method and order. Old John kept his accounts on the backs of envelopes or in his head. Young John might have swings of mood, but Old John sank into abysms from which it seemed he could never be rescued. When a friend died of pneumonia, "Father had an awful cold on his lungs next day," and while a neighbor lay critically ill, "Father's physical condition was one of general collapse."

"I notice this about Father, Julia, that he does not go at his work with the snap which he doubtless did when he was a younger man. He has always liked to put off until tomorrow what did not have to be done today, and the habit seems to be growing on him."

Nevertheless, the senior partner could come in at his leisurely eleven o'clock, and in ten minutes produce the case for which the junior partner had searched eight hours. "He is a tower of strength to me," John wrote, and when he heard in a roundabout way that his father had spoken of him as a help, he was genuinely and ingenuously delighted.

Like the rest of the family, Young John derived a certain entertainment from the spectacle of Father doing exactly as he pleased, in his invariable way.

"He surreptitiously bought and brought home another monster St. Bernard dog, against the silent and frowning disapproval of the whole family, and with great shamefacedness on his part. I am a crank on dogs, Father is a monomaniac. We assert that his chief love is for his dogs, then for his new $250 buggy, then for his wife and children. There is a hint of slander in the saying.

"Father has his foibles, which anyone can see, but I admire and love him more than any man I know, and I don't begrudge him anything that will lighten his burdens."

Still John W. could not pluck up the courage to talk to John J. about the engagement. He cravenly suggested that Father must know it anyway, since he saw so many letters coming in and going out. He did confide in his mother, who took it well, and then in Emma, "dear good girl," who was pleased. Nan, as usual, said the wrong thing.

The months dragged on. Occasionally John managed a night or two at Media. Julia thought it would be improper for her to visit Clarksburg. Then the situation was saved from monotony by a new excitement. In the autumn of 1898, friends urged John to run for the legislature. He reacted as he reacted to every suggestion of public office throughout his life. He did not want the nomination, would make no effort for it, would not consider it, would not take it. He had no political ambitions. "I have urged my enthusiastic friends to let me alone, and I think I have them sufficiently dampened down. My set is sot."

When he was nominated anyway, he ran scared. "I have a Republican majority of five hundred to overcome, and that is no easy matter, because it means that in every speech I have to leave the Republicans in a good humour and yet content the Democrats. I am not a spell binder, and I leave no one hoarse from over-cheering, but they all listen intently."

Much as he hated it, he made more speeches than anyone on either side because his partner on the ticket refused to speak at all. No hamlet in a hollow escaped his visit, and if he could not reach it in a buggy, he went on horseback. He spent a night in a log cabin with a family of eleven, while his host entertained him with jigs on the fiddle. He went down into the mines to shake hands with the miners, wishing that he had time to do more of it because that was the kind of electioneering that counted. He went out to the tunnel and shook hands with the Irish. "I like the Irish, for all you can't depend on what they say."

"It is not so much that I want to be elected," he explained to Julia, "as that I hate to be licked. If any chance to climb slips by me, it will have to go by in the dark, or be too dubious to repay the chasing."

He wrote her on election eve. "By the morrow both the sanguine reporters and the pessimistic prophets will have rested from their labors, and I am glad of it. I have not time for a real letter tonight, dearest, because some politicians are waiting to see me."

He was elected, and by a good majority.

At once he threw himself into preparing for the new responsibility. "I keep a list of every bill which a constituent wishes me to introduce, and some of them are odd indeed, but they show what the people want." When he was mentioned for the speakership he thought it might interfere with his chance to make a reputation on the floor. "I am not going to become a politician, but I do not want to spoil my chances for running for whatever I might want in future." He got a copy of the Rules to study. "Good parliamentarians will be in demand."

And also: "Julia, if you desire it, I will speak to Father about our plans before I go to Charleston. Will do it if it kills me, and I expect it will."

Father took the surprise calmly, merely remarking that if Miss Julia resembled her mother all would be well, for Mrs. McDonald, whom he had once met, was one of the most charming women both in manner and appearance he had ever seen.

So Julia had to resign herself to being engaged to a public man. With her intense feeling for family life, she had dreaded the plunge into politics, but she took it gracefully.

"To think that I fell in love with a West Virginia pedagogue, and now he is so famous and everyone heaping honours upon him! I just see you continuing in politics in spite of all you say and all I say. You can't resist the people, and they need you. So you can make up your mind to be the champion of all that is just and good. No one can take more heartfelt interest in all your undertakings than your adoring Julia."

From the legislature John wrote his father that he had never dreamed there were so many varieties of rascality. His first fight was against a fraudulent roll of members sent in by the West Virginia secretary of state. He won his battle to get the frauds turned out, and seemed able to make even his enemies like him. "As long as I keep my head and don't talk too much I can be the leader of the floor on our side of the house. Tomorrow the enemy will hammer me to a fare-you-well, so sympathize with your soon to be obliterated John." He became the floor leader, and newspapers referred to him as "the boy orator." "All the kind things said make me feel like a boy in a new suit of tight clothes."

Cautiously, he began to think that he might be able to support a wife, although as late as April he was still denying rumors. Julia laughed at him. "It amuses me, John, that you are still trying to fool your townspeople. You might as well own up that you have put your foot in it."

At last the six-year-old secret was out, June set for the wedding. John's mother, sincerely delighted, wrote a charming letter to her prospective daughter-in-law.

We are all ready to open the doors of our hearts to you, and hope you may find some vacant corners in yours for us. As for John, he is simply walking on air with his head striking the stars. For some time no arithmetic could convince him that you might not starve if you married him, but now that it is settled, he declines a three thousand dollar salary as below the reach of his ambition. Give my love to your mother especially, and tell her that only she herself can love and care for her little girl better than I will try to do.

With tenderest love,
Anna Davis.

The young couple agreed to live with the Davises for a few weeks or months after the wedding. Houses to rent in Clarksburg were scarce and undesirable, boarding impossible; besides, John had bought a lot and wished to save every penny toward building.

"I expect to be as happy as a big sunflower," Julia told him. "I know, John, that we cannot sit on a rainbow and eat honey all day, but when difficulties come we will face them together. I'm sure we will love one another so devotedly that it will be a pleasure to do what is most convenient and agreeable to the other."

Although John dreaded a big church wedding, he tried to live up to this idea by agreeing to go through with it if Julia wished. In fact, he was so eager to marry her that she could set her own terms, *within reason.* He would even wear *white gloves.* ("A dress suit after six o'clock, says Harper's Bazaar.")

"I want you to know, there is no getting out of it now, although how the Medians are to get along without my Julia I don't see, for if there was ever a sweeter or more useful or more indispensable girl under any roof, the fact is not recorded."

"Your humble slave," John signed himself, then could not quite go through with it. "Slave with a string tied to it, but yours to count on. Your wise, strong, yet tender nature is the best of earthly comforts to all who know you."

At Media the family rejoiced determinedly, not without tears. "Mama weeps every time I try to talk to her, and Papa never alludes to it, but, John, we can't go on forever as we are now. It's what our fathers and mothers have done before us. When I told Percy this might be our last winter together, we both had a good cry! He's a darling boy and has been as much in my life as he says I've been to him. I only hope we will be as successful in homemaking as Mama and Papa have been. Unselfishness is the foundation. When I want to be a bear, you will have to forbear."

John made some suggestions which Julia vetoed. She turned down the new fad of twin beds. Also, "I would do most anything you asked me, dear, but it is indeed too much to 'spar' with you at night like your Fairmont friend. I suggest your investing in a punching bag instead of a pair of boxing gloves." (John bought the gloves and Julia learned to use them.)

She went trousseau shopping in Washington. "I am going to have the most snatching silk dress and black picture hat you ever saw. We took a big bottle of wine for refreshment when the day's work was done, and lost half of it in our trunk! I've had enough bouquets thrown at me to turn a poor girl's head.

It's well one doesn't marry often—but then it's the novelty of the thing that brings out the flattery."

She confided her qualms about the great change coming in her life to an aunt, who assured her that all brides felt as if they were stepping off the earth.

Work piled on John until he feared he might have only two days for his honeymoon. At the last his father stayed away from the wedding to handle the affairs of a client. "That's the good thing about having a partner who knows twice as much as you do. We have some big fish on the line now, sweetheart, and must not treat them like minnows."

At Media the cook left, and Julia took over. "To think I have waited six years to marry the McDonald's cook! But I'll do it and be the proudest man alive."

My darling Julia, my very last letter to you as my sweetheart, for tomorrow I leave to meet you face to face. As you, Julia, are my first, I have no other wish than that you should be my only love.

Your very happy,
John.

On a June afternoon, while the late sun drew its golden patterns under the oaks, John and Julia were married on the lawn at Media before a homemade altar covered with country flowers. The children made an aisle of daisy chains, the bridesmaids in green organdie carried sweet peas which the bride had planted, the honeysuckle gave its incense. No ceremony could have been more in accord with the spirit of the bride.

"If aught but death part thee and me, John, nothing else shall."

And John, who had protested that he had had no time to be scared, felt perfectly calm, not even excited, took his wife to a hotel in Washington for their wedding night and forgot to write her name in the registry. The clerk had to inquire who the lady was.

Into the dark and quiet house at Clarksburg, Julia brought warmth and laughter. She and John sang together, or made music with violin and piano. The Davises unanimously adored her, and the visit lasted for months, although the bride felt that she did not have enough to do.

When she mentioned this in a letter, the Major, who had strong ideas on wifely duty, hastened to dash off some good advice in his nervous, racing hand.

"If you will just look about you, you will see small things which can be done for other members of the household, and keep yourself busy that way—but why should I tell you to do what you have been doing over since you were born? I know that you will be the blessing to your new family that you have always been to us."

She was not to complain of late and irregular meals, "for there are times when meals must wait on business and you must submit to it with a good grace." Since John had to take so many trips, it was better for her to be with the family than alone in a house. And Papa made Mama write her that she must go first to the Presbyterian church with the Davises and *afterwards* to the Episcopalian, advice which Mrs. McDonald could not give without reservations.

"I know that you will always *be* an Episcopalian, because you were born one, but you had better do as Papa says. He was quite cross with me because I had not mentioned it to you."

In spite of the Major's determination that she should make a good wife, he had to admit that they missed her at Media. "Your life with us is a sweet memory. I called you Birdie because your infant life was as bright and songful as a woodland bird, and years have only made those notes richer and the name dearer. You were a precious charge, and the keeping of it brought much happiness to the household. With both my Julias out of the house it is lonely to me. I was never lonesome in my life before." He knew his duty, however, and concluded stoutly, "your marriage to a devoted faithful husband I regard as our chief blessing."

Her mother said the same in her own way. "We can never get used to your absence. It seems the more you stay away the more we want to see you. Foolish fondness, when we know that you have your heart's desire, and it is well with you both to be together."

Percy was more direct and less conscience ridden. "We miss you so much in everything, Jule. Angus said the place did not seem the same." Angus added his voice. "John has got you through the tears and with the smiles of all of us. May this be the happiest Christmas in your short and beautiful life. If you remain the same Julia you have always been to us and to everyone else, I'm sure no one, not even John, could raise any objections."

In addition to missing Julia, the family at Media went through much sadness during that year. Mrs. McDonald's father died, and although she was "thankful to have him at peace and in heaven, yet the love of a lifetime seems to yearn for its object." Soon after, her sister Mary died, leaving four small children, and then her brother Will, leaving a child unborn. Julia was sobered by these deaths.

"I hope my dear husband may be spared to me for many years, and that we can go together when the time comes."

To satisfy her longing for a home of her own, she and John briefly rented a friend's house, but by then "little Johnny" was on the way, she did not feel well and it seemed best for her to spend the month of May at Media, "beloved place, beloved people. The country air, how different it is!" She would return to the welcoming Davises for the birth, and in the autumn she and John would move into the house which they were building. The plans had been drawn, the foundations started. After all, they would have the rest of their lives to keep house together. The Major wrote, "your aunt considers your anxiety to go to housekeeping a form of insanity. Learn to labor and to wait."

Julia found it good to be at Media, although now with a divided heart.

"Ten months ago today we were married. It seems a short time, and yet I feel as if I had always been married to you! Oh the difference this ten months have made! How our lives have grown together. We seem daily to get more and more absorbed in one another and think alike. I've been away as long as I can stand it, and want to get back to my good old man. I am never going to leave you again, no never."

John saw nothing good in her absence and hurried down to visit her whenever his work permitted. "If ever a trip paid for itself this one did. I can't live without you, and that's a fact. I'm a ruint man and can't be happy anymore without my Babener. You'll never know how much self-denial your absence has cost me. If you hadn't been sweet and good, B.B. with such a mother to pattern from, you would have evinced more than your share of original sin."

The visits could not be frequent, however, for his work claimed him more and more. "I figure that yesterday I worked fifteen hours solid. This world with all its skulduggery is an extremely amusing place to be in." When he could stand the separation no longer, he went down and brought her back.

In late June her mother came to be with her in Clarksburg, but the baby did not arrive as expected. After a month, Julia felt embarrassed at keeping Mama away from the family for so long. On the night of the birth the family doctor was incapacitated and another man had to be hastily summoned.

It was an instrument birth, but at first all seemed well. Mrs. McDonald wrote her husband that she would stay on a few days to make sure. "But I thank God for a strong constitution that never required any aid except a Negro Mammy and a kettle of hot water."

Since the baby had not succeeded in being little Johnny, Julia decided to name it Anna Kennedy after her much loved mother-in-law.

Then an infection from unsterilized instruments made its appearance. Puerperal fever set in. For three agonizing weeks the struggle continued. The family hoped and dreaded, hoped and again lost hope. At last nothing more could be done.

They brought Julia her daughter. "Dear little Anna Kennedy," she said. Her eyes went to her husband. "Don't cry, John. I'm going to fight it out."

The rest is silence.

II

So began my divided life between the high silent house and the open sunny one. So too began my close acquaintance with many good soldiers in the regiment of life, all devoted to training the new recruit. My situation seemed normal to me because I knew nothing else.

I might have stayed uninterruptedly with the Davises, converged on and directed by a household of much older people, but my father would not have it. He rarely made suggestions as to my behavior, since he perceived that I lived under a running fire of suggestions, but on one point he was firm. I must spend a large part of every summer at Media, and I must be left there alone as soon as I grew old enough not to burden that busy household. He thought that the McDonalds had something valuable to give me, and he was right.

The growing years are the long years. Then surroundings, minutely observed, begin to emerge from the haze of infancy and take on character. Then the adult giants gradually become human beings with individuality of their own.

At first I seem to have known each of the family in Clarksburg by a single trait. Grandfather was the atmosphere in which we moved and breathed. He had created our house, he pervaded it, he set the tone. In my early memory that house seemed as living an entity as the people, and he and the house were one. Grandmother was at first a lap, Aunt Emma a pair of hands, Aunt Nan, at one remove, a block away, a voice. Only much later did I see them as they really were, rather than as they were in relation to *me*.

Quite literally, I owe my life to Anna Kennedy, whose namesake I never became. She solved the feeding problems which followed my mother's death. During the first year she wrote weekly to the other grandmother about "your baby," describing the formulas patiently tried and rejected, the encouraging signs of mental normalcy in spite of the battered head, the final discarding of doctors for a brave experiment with cow's milk, which succeeded.

"She woke at five, and there began a struggle between the baby who wanted to get up and the grandmother who did not. At five thirty I gave in. I look forward to the day when I can tell her about her dear mother, and teach her to love our precious one."

When I was finally out of danger, the letters took on a triumphant tone. "I can't make you understand our baby unless you see her. She rarely cries, never frets, but wants her own way. If she is doing something she shouldn't, we hear her saying to herself, 'Naughty Juja'. Then when she is caught, she laughs. I'm afraid she thinks, perhaps with reason, that anything can be bought with kisses."

By the time I was nearly two, it is evident that Grandmother had learned to love me because I had given her so much trouble.

"She can repeat nursery rhymes, recognize capital letters, and has some idea of numbers. We are not urging her development too much, but the fact is we can't help it, she is so alert. Now there! For once I have given myself full swing and lauded our baby to the skies, and if you think it is funny, why you must laugh."

A year later: "Emma is her favorite. Of course she does not require much lifting now, but then I cannot lift her at all."

And the year after that: "Alas for the discipline I had counted on. I have gone back in the most craven fashion to the old 'sweet reasonableness', although I never did like too much sugar in anything."

My father, stunned and despairing, was content to leave me in her hands. His conscientious efforts at what has come to be repulsively called "togetherness," were not conspicuously successful. He had no talent for holding babies.

He too made his reports to Mrs. McDonald. "The rare occasions when I am bold enough to try to hold her are signalized by a vigorous and instantaneous protest. The undutiful young lady seems to have determined that of all her train I am least to her liking. I long for the day when there will be something I can do for her."

It may be that my small body could feel even then in his arms the rigidity of his shyness, the inflexible sorrow which lay on his heart.

He threw himself into his work as another man might have

sought oblivion in drink. "My work is so much a comfort to me. The only time when I can shake off my sorrowful memories is when I am plunged deep in business. I would not forget for a kingdom, and yet my memories are more than I can bear. If Julia had been left behind she would have continued bravely. I can do no less. As for the baby, only God knows what the preservation and continuance of her life means to me."

His hours grew longer, his trips more frequent, his return to the office after dinner invariable. He was always kindly, often abstracted, but I knew then, and I know still, that looking at me hurt his heart.

I was aware, however, of his intense devotion, aware that he belonged to me in a way that not even my grandmother did. He was remote, and given to appearances like the gods of Olympus, but unlike the gods, his favors were not capricious. He loved me steadily, and I loved him as one loves a god, with an aching wish for greater unity.

Like the gods, also, he was the source of every blessing. From him came the pony which threw and kicked me, the school which I enjoyed but little, the toys to which I was so indifferent that I used to throw them out of the third-story window to watch them spin down through the trees. What I wanted from him was his time, and he had little to spare.

"If I had anything to do with this child," he would say, "she should do so and so—but of course she is not mine."

His mother yearned over her son in the years of his sorrow. I once overheard a sentence, spoken with such passionate feeling that it has stayed with me forever, although I cannot remember when or where I heard it, or to whom she was speaking.

"If I could have taken her place in the grave and brought her back to my son, I would have done so gladly."

She wrote to Mrs. McDonald—they were too Victorian ever

to reach a first name basis—"My poor boy has gotten out his violin again. I was glad to see it, but I suppose one thing hurts no more than another when all the heart is full of one pain. . . . We go about in our unfortunate reserved family way, with our hearts aching for ourselves and each other, but with few words, and fewer tears. So I catch only an occasional glimpse of John's inner life. Can't you bear to come this fall? I know it will bring it all back, but you cannot always stay away, and we are all treading together the via dolorosa of memory this month. I wish you could see your baby. She is the most affectionate little soul."

Grandmother McDonald never came, but her replies were frequent, fond, interested, and gracefully expressed. Only once did her emotions run away with her pen. "Oh, if the babe knew what she had cost us, she would never smile again!"

I cannot say from direct recollection what was in my father's heart during those first years. Every Easter for the rest of his life he wrote asking to have flowers put in the churchyard, "for the beloved dust which sleeps there. There is nothing left for me except to try to live worthily as the man she loved."

The Clarksburg house had ceased to be a home to him. It was the garden of his sorrow, the mount of his affliction, and he stayed out of it when he could. Of course, this did not prevent me from enjoying it very much.

Grandfather Davis felt that he had set up a permanent refuge for his descendants. He could, and even did, speak of home in these terms:

> The fire burns brightest on one's own hearth. The lost diamond knows no difference between the dust where it lies and the bosom from which it fell, but all that has vitality requires a home—a home which along the conduits of memory may bear pure nourishment to children and the children's children, so long as it shall stand, and after it has fallen.

Twelve years and six children after his marriage, he built the house for his family. He paid one thousand dollars for his lot, got out his ruler and drew the plans himself: a long hall down the middle; front and back parlor on one side; steep stairs jammed in between the library and the dining room; curved lines not necessary.

Some houses sit, but 303 Lee Street stood, in the midst of two acres, surrounded by noble trees and taller than they. Clarksburg lies in a cup of the West Virginia hills, but level sites can be found at the east and west ends of the town. Grandfather preferred to be a block from his office and the courthouse, and go straight up in the air.

A wall at the foot of the lot kept it from sliding into the street. There were steps at the gate, steps from one terrace to another on the front walk, thirteen steps between wide balustrades sweeping up to the porch. In icy weather the trip inspired caution. Aunt Emma broke three ribs once, but most of us were more fortunate.

Above the columns of the porch the tall windows of the second story commanded a wide view. Higher still peered the dormers of the third, crowned by a black slate roof sloping to four towering chimneys. Over the middle window in the third story brooded a large tin ornament with curved sides like praying angels, known as the cherubim and seraphim because in a wind they continually did cry.

The kitchen, an afterthought, was tacked on the rear, and the back stairs jutted out by the dining-room door to catch the ankles of the unwary on the long run from coal range to table. These back stairs had been a problem to the amateur architect. It proved necessary to hitch them to the second floor by slicing a circular section out of Aunt Nan's room and installing some extra steps.

A home needed no closets, "holes in which women collect

trash." (This from Grandfather, who never threw away even an envelope!) In each bedroom there stood a wardrobe large enough to play house in, but so constructed that a woman's dress could not hang at full length. One bathroom of uncertain performance was tucked in over the kitchen, where Grandfather could and did ignore it, preferring until his death the tin hat tub which the "outside man" placed in front of his fire and filled with hot water. He never gave up his coal fire. Coal, which he did not carry up, was more healthful than gas, and soot, which he did not clear away, did not matter. He also found it better for his eyes to read always by an oil lamp which Aunt Emma filled and trimmed for him.

Grandmother called the house a woman-killer, but since she was seventy-five when she said that, the house had evidently taken its time.

It is fair to admit that Grandfather was no architect, but he secured sound workmanship. Even the interior partitions were twelve inches of solid brick, a fact which made it impossible to install central heating later on. The slate roof needed no repairs in eighty years; the banisters survived three generations of sliding children without a quiver. Like its builder, the house made no compromises. Integrity came before grace.

Three of us lived there with my grandparents—my unmarried Aunt Emma, occasionally my father, and myself. Aunt Nan had married a year after my birth and moved a block away.

Grandfather made our climate one of fervent rectitude, frequent agitation, occasional despair. Grandmother brought us through the storms. To his wild swings of temperament she opposed an immovable calm. She was the small but solid rock on which her children rested.

Nevertheless, he and she delayed not to disagree upon everything, from card playing (which she enjoyed, and which he thought suspect if not sinful), to the nature of the Trinity. When World War I broke out she almost drove him to be pro-German by coming out strongly on the Allied side. Their contests were neither petty nor personal; their subjects national and sometimes cosmic. They did not hope to convince each other—they had been too long acquainted for that—but each liked to sharpen the mind on a worthy antagonist.

Almost daily I heard the beautiful voice of my Grandfather ringing out over his late breakfast. (He claimed that no client worth having ever came to a man's office before eleven.) Grandmother rose at six, worked in her garden, set the household in order, breakfasted at eight with the rest of the family, freed herself for intellectual work. At ten thirty she came to keep him company, along with Tristan, the Great Dane, and Pluto, the Saint Bernard, of whose presence in the house she did not approve.

"No no, Anna, I shall not be silent. I shall take my stand. The chief duty of a good citizen is to be angry when anger is called for; to withstand the multitude hasting to do evil. I shall abide by the Democratic party so long as it is the party of the people and no longer."

I sidled in to watch the show. "How are you this morning, Grandfather?"

Over his mustache cup he gave me the usual answer. "Far from well." Then, on a really sepulchral level, "*Far* from well."

Having voiced his alarm, he took another bite of his waffle laced with chicken hash, or his buckwheat cakes with New Orleans molasses, or his flannel cakes and beef hash with dumplings, and returned to his argument, shaking a bony finger at Grandmother as if she were personally responsible for all that he disliked in the state of the world.

"Look about you, Anna. I tell you, the Democratic party is now a mere heterogeneous aggregation of discordant elements, without any recognizable leadership, and fatally bent on self-destruction."

"Last night you said the Republicans were worse."

"So they are!" Grandfather exclaimed, not at all pleased to be reminded of it. "An oligarchy of millionaires, whose lives have been devoted to the sordid worship of wealth—the Rockefeller-Morgan-Hill combination, Wall Street and all that Wall Street stands for in the way of special privilege and greed, has drawn its slimy folds around democracy and is crushing the life out of it. Any body of men associated politically for any purpose other than to maintain principles is no better than a band of spoilsmen bound together for plunder. There must be a parting of the ways in this country between Constitutional Government, and the forces of Plutocracy, Imperialism, and Materialism."

He was plainly rehearsing the speech which he had to give that night, well launched on a favorite theme, his voice gathering power, his white beard quivering, his violet eyes blazing, his finger driving home his points. Grandmother, a plump little monolith, her hair combed up in white silk wings from her pink face, her china-blue eyes gleaming behind gold-rimmed spectacles, waited for the moment to puncture the balloon and bring it down.

"I suppose, John, we have to be governed by one party or the other."

Grandfather did not choose to consider this. "Pshaw, Anna, I shall not tamely submit. The spirit of materialism is the Angel of Pestilence dropping the seeds of death from its black wing wherever it sweeps." He paused to be pleased with his metaphor, then sailed grandly on. "You can see it in this town. People from *Ohio*, from *Pennsylvania*, from God knows where, flocking in since oil was struck. Low people, Anna. I tell you, they are *low* people. They think only of *money*." The last word he enunciated with blood-chilling contempt. Then all the stops came out, the organ rolled. "Plain living and high thinking are no more!"

He had some justification for his view. Clarksburg was rowdy. I was forbidden to walk on Pike Street, where the swinging doors of the saloons were interrupted only by the closed doors of more mysterious establishments. When I did it anyway, I was rewarded by seeing a man knocked through a saloon door to lie unconscious on the pavement. Well accustomed, under a complexity of direction, to keeping my own counsel, I did not report this incident at home.

"Perhaps, John, we should move away." Grandmother sometimes exhibited a satiric turn of mind.

"It is no better elsewhere," Grandfather said hastily. "The Republic is staggering to its fall from the rottenness in its vitals. We are treading in the footsteps of Egypt, Babylon, and Rome, in the ruins of whose once glorious palaces the serpent crawls as king."

But Grandmother was not taking a lecture on the Roman Empire. "Yet you class women with minors, paupers, and those of unsound mind. There is inequality for you!"

Checked in mid-flight, Grandfather glared at her.

"Stuff and nonsense, Anna. To give women the vote would merely enlarge the electorate, make politics more unwieldy, and affect the outcome not a whit."

"John, that is not responsive to what I said."

Faced by those calm keen eyes, Grandfather could not assert his belief that women did not have the mentality for the problems of government. He snorted.

"I hope I shall not live to see it."

"I think you will, John."

This was too much. With a trembling hand he poured his coffee into his saucer to cool, drank it, and left for the office.

His daughter Emma, who liked doing things for people, handed him his hat and cane at the front door. I heard him say, in not too low a mutter, "Em, your mother is mulish. She is *mulish*, Em."

Grandmother rose, unperturbed. "Come along, my girlie. It is time for your lessons." She led me upstairs, calling back over her shoulder, "Em, get the dogs out of the house."

Going upstairs with Grandmother for lessons was the routine of my day. Until I was nine, she taught me at home, as she had taught each of her children.

I have said that I remember her first as a lap. It was not then the fashion for women of sixty to look (approximately) like girls, and I can testify that for a small child nothing is so comforting as a deep bosom. On that warm lap, rocking in front of a coal fire, I was sung to sleep with old hymns and lullabies, my small aches healed with nonsense rhymes.

Oh Grandmother what a pain I got.
Take me to the 'pothecary's shop,
Give me nasty medicine, don't care what,
Just so it cure this pain I got.

Be it remembered, however, that Grandmother was not a woman to wallow in sentiment. That same lap soon became my schoolroom. She shared her interests with me.

A *History of Egypt* by Maspero in thirteen red volumes was too heavy for me to hold. Grandmother held me and the books as well, and made such funny comments about the queer one-sided people that I demanded it again and again. Unfortunately I have lost the turn of this wit, but Isis, Osiris, Rameses, and the rest became good friends.

We were not always stuck in the past. We also followed the doings of the Sunbonnet Babies, where I learned to recognize a word at a time. It was a method she had invented herself. Later it became general and, I understand, suited to some children and not to others. It suited me. By the time I was four, I could read what I pleased.

Spelling came from remembering how words looked. Writing was harder, but after making rows of pothooks, J, and coathangers, ſ, it turned out to be copying words again. Then we reached arithmetic, and the end of my reputation as a bright baby.

Again and again the buttons from her button box were laid out on the floor, patiently combined and recombined. Some of them were pretty and interesting, particularly one with tiny steel flowers on purple velvet, but I could not care how many were left when four were removed. Once she stood me in a corner until three times seven was dredged from my subconscious. It has become the peg from which I hang the multiplication tables. Apparently I should have stood in the corner more often.

"Pay attention. You are not paying attention. I could let your father turn somersaults and he would still know what he was doing, but if I don't make you sit in one place, your mind flutters off like a butterfly. If you pay attention, you will see how it is."

Not all was cuddling on those soft round knees. Once I was swiftly spanked across them. I had slapped her, and she did not like it. Probably I had been inattentive, this led to restraint, restraint to rebellion, and rebellion was promptly put down. It seems a logical sequence, and Grandmother was logical before all else.

She did not give way to discouragement over my shortcomings. Day after day and every day, without the slightest flagging on her part, she taught me reading, writing, arithmetic (if I can be said to have learned it), piano, and *Little Arthur's History of England*, a delightful volume which reduced the kings and queens of England to good or bad boys and girls.

"Richard II was not so well brought up as he should have been. . . . I think you will like Henry V. . . . Queen Elizabeth did not find it easy to undo all the mischief that Queen Mary had done." American history was summed up in a single page. "It was not wonderful that the Americans beat out the English soldiers, who did not like to be sent so far from Home to fight against men who spoke the same language as themselves."

There were holes in this painless educational system. I must have been six or seven when an elderly gentleman stopped me on the hill and asked if I knew the alphabet. I did not. I never learned it until I began looking up words in the dictionary, but I still remember the shame of being thought a dunce.

Grandmother had fought her battle for the budding mind four times before. (Two of her children died in infancy.) She brought each of us along as fast as we could travel. Fortunately, she had never heard of making a child "unadjusted to his contemporaries" or "unrelated to his group." She held the view that since no one could live long enough to learn all there was to know, the tiresome groundwork should be covered as soon as possible. Fundamentally, it is hard to disagree with this.

Of course we were all ahead of ourselves when we finally reached school, which caused a passing awkwardness, but herd life soon fell into place. We had all learned to enjoy stretching our mental powers, and one and all we knew something about Paying Attention.

Nor did she abandon us when we left her knee. The spur and the keen interest followed on.

Herself one of the first women in the country to receive a B.A., she could not send her daughters to college, partly because of their father's ideas and partly because of financial insufficiencies. She did what she could for them.

"Lillie was never so tired of winter and the monotony of life here." She got Lillie off to teach school in Lewisburg, where she met her husband.

Nannie was the problem child, too much imagination, too little direction. "She is doing well at school, but gets into her usual tantrums over her arithmetic and algebra." "Nannie is at work in earnest, or as much so as usual." "Nannie is under the weather today. Threatened with cholera, she says. She always has an ache or a pain on hand, you know." And finally, "Nannie seems ready for anything in the way of a sensation."

Something must be arranged for Nannie. She contrived to have her take a kindergarten course and start a school in the basement.

Emma could draw, so the struggle was to have her study art in Baltimore. First she was sent there to visit her Aunt Emma.

"I get lonely for you, little girl, but I wish that you could stay and take lessons. When I speak to your Papa about it, he doesn't say a word, and leaves pretty soon."

"Send word about expenses at the Maryland Institute *right away*. If you put it off the tide will turn again, and you will miss your chance. It happens to look favorable just now because Mrs. Young was here last night and asked if you could teach freehand drawing from nature, etc. Of course I told her that you could teach nothing but crayon from copy and a little freehand, and I think it opened your father's eyes to the state of the case. Or at least called his attention to it."

"I do not quite give up hope. If only I could get five minutes' talk with your father. He is always flying about. In Weston today."

Wifely arts prevailed in the end. Emma had not one, but two terms at the Institute.

The heart of Grandmother's life, however, not expressed but perfectly clear to everyone, was her son. Her letters never went farther in affection than "Dear John," and "Your loving

Mother," but no one could miss the glow of cautious pride which emanates from the pages.

She labored to form his mind. Every unnecessary word was pared from his early compositions. "You are taking the life out of it," Grandfather protested. "No, John. I am trying to teach him to be clear and concise."

When she reluctantly sent him to school at nine, she did not cease to watch over his progress.

"Johnny has been lazy as usual, and his average is only a fraction over 92. I am afraid the stimulus of school is wearing off. I have been trying to spur him up a little."

(Idle Johnny! Only 92! Where is that miracle of scholarly diligence who was held up to me as a model?)

He went to college as a matter of course; no need to fight a battle there. When he graduated, she wrote to her son-in-law, Mr. Preston (whom she never called anything else), about a job for him. The letter is a model of understatement.

"I do not think John is brilliant, but I am sure he will work as hard as any man alive."

Then it was my turn to be spurred on, idle Julia, like the rest. "What is the matter with your algebra? Only a B." "I can't believe your German is as feeble as you say. What is the matter? Too many outside interests I suppose." Yet when I failed three out of seven College Board examinations, there were no reproaches, only a forward-looking rearrangement of plans.

It was her goal to see each of her children develop to the utmost. Her efforts brought her another reward as well. Her children adored her. After her death each one in turn took occasion to say to me, "Mother once told me that in some ways I was more like her than any child she had."

She was as ambitious for me as for the rest. She did not have to urge my father to send me to college, but that was not enough. She would have liked me to study for a profession. One day she asked me what I wished to be in life.

I knew without hesitation. "A good wife and mother."

"Is that *all?*"

What else could I wish, with her example before me? I wanted to be loved as she had been loved.

III

My dissimilar grandparents met when Anna Kennedy came out from Baltimore to be bridesmaid for a school friend in Clarksburg. It was then a remote country town, oil unheard of and coal a fuel to be scratched out of an open vein in the hillside. The townsfolk carried their own lanterns to light them over the unpaved streets. As the wedding party went from one house to another, a tall young man offered Miss Kennedy his arm in the darkness. Teasing, she lifted her lantern to peer at him.

"Let's see what you look like."

That look changed the world for both of them.

She was a tiny thing, less than five feet tall, who could walk under his arm in the heelless slippers then fashionable, who wore her hair in ringlets down her cheeks, who laughed easily, and had to be carried over mud puddles. He may well have thought that he was acquiring a doll, a toy, a charm for his watch chain. It was not so.

In their fifty-six years of contest, no win on either side,

Grandfather was master of the house, but Grandmother was mistress of herself.

Their arguments began in their first love letters. He was not a church member, and she devoutly worried about his salvation. He wished to preserve the Union, she rashly hung out a Confederate flag. He did not believe in educating females, she had taken a B.A. at the Woman's College in Baltimore in 1858. (Her great-granddaughter asked me if it was for china painting and needlework. No, it was in Latin, Greek, and higher mathematics.)

By the time I knew them, they had changed sides. John was an elder, in fact *the* elder, in a particularly bleak little southern Presbyterian church. Anna taught free-thinking courses in the exegesis of the Bible which would have appalled him had he ever attended. He fought rabidly for States' Rights; she thought the growth of Federal power inevitable.

When they were married they traveled to Clarksburg on the last train over the Baltimore and Ohio railroad before the Confederates tore up the tracks. In the fashion of the day, the entire wedding party accompanied them as far as Cumberland.

The babies arrived with Victorian regularity, Lillie the first year, Em the next, then Moselle, who died in infancy, then Nan, then John, then Estelle. Domestic duties, which bored Mrs. Davis, were unremitting, accomplishments had to be laid aside. Her diploma hung behind a door, her early oil paintings adorned the parlor, but no others followed them. Her music, from Liszt to "The Maiden's Prayer," lay in a recess under the stairs.

When they moved into the new house before it was finished, she contracted pneumonia wading around the flooded cellar which was first used for a kitchen. It proved serious. Lying in what her attendants thought a coma, she heard the doctor say,

"John, she is gone." She felt herself out in a black space, and fighting, fighting to come back. She came back.

"Galloping consumption" followed the pneumonia. For this the accepted cure was to immure the patient in a hot airless room. This treatment brought the end quickly, and Anna's mother, two sisters, and a brother had succumbed to it. When the doctor, after the stern manner of the time, gave her the opportunity to make her peace with God by telling her that she could not live until spring, she believed him; but, looking at her young children, she thought that she must see them grow up.

Against medical head shaking and too weak to walk, she had her husband lift her into the buggy every afternoon. For an hour or so, in all weathers, they drove slowly around the countryside, while he held her in his arms. She recovered. Furthermore, none of her children contracted the disease, although constantly exposed to "deadly night air," with open windows.

During her child-rearing years the pace was hard, but her inner rebellion expressed itself only in migraine headaches. To Emma at boarding school she wrote, "I was forty-two on Saturday. I think you were the only one who remembered my birthday. I am getting old. Lillie is always scolding about my wrinkles. She says I frown all the time. That is neuralgia though. It seems there is never less to do no matter how much is done." Then she added the inevitable prod. "I can't say I think your report a brilliant one. Your spelling is sad. 88!"

A deep grief almost overwhelmed her when her youngest, Estelle, died at six of scarlet fever. I heard so much about Estelle that she became for me an imaginary playmate, a fairy child, the prettiest, the brightest, the most loving, embalmed in her perpetual youth, her timeless innocence. Grandmother was not one to dwell on sorrow, but one evening, swinging on the front porch while the fireflies lit the grass, she gave me an unforgettable confidence.

"After Estelle died, I once found myself in the cemetery without knowing how I had come there, and trying to dig up the grave with a sharp stick. When I realized what I was doing, I turned myself around and came home. I have never given way like that over anything again."

Through it all she found time for intellectual life as one finds time to eat and drink. On the Easter morning when John was born, she was reading Gibbon's *Decline and Fall of the Roman Empire* and made the doctor wait until she finished the chapter.

She founded study clubs which covered everything from Greek drama to the history of philosophy, endowing at least one of them with such vitality that it is still extant. When she had a paper to write, she would send to the Peabody Library in Baltimore for ten or twenty volumes and open the package with the expression of a child on Christmas morning. Everyone in Clarksburg who had an interest in the life of the mind came sooner or later to talk to Grandmother in the front parlor. In memory I see her most clearly with a book in a big chair, her back against one arm, her small feet dangling over the other.

She did not preach to us on the pleasure of acquiring knowledge. We had her example. One year she took up Hebrew with an erudite Catholic priest; during her seventieth winter, confined to her room by illness, she amused herself by learning to read Dante in the original; two months before she died, she was studying Spanish. "*Don Quixote* is going well, but my grammar does not stand examination. It is fortunate that my living does not depend on my capacity to study. I read and read, and forget and forget."

In a teasing way which deceived nobody, Grandfather took pride in her, all the more since his own education had been sketchy. He began life a shy country boy in a family of artisans, a clockmaker, a silversmith, a harness maker. His father took no interest in educating him until an unmarried aunt pressed the cause after he won a gold watch as a Latin prize. In the end he was grudgingly permitted, not to go to college, but to read law with Judge Brockenbrough at Washington College, later Washington and Lee. Perhaps as an outcome of these early frustrations, he had the most useless hands I ever saw, long, thin, totally incapable; hands which he passed on to my father.

When he completed his course, he came home, rented an office, and for several days sat in it with the shades pulled down for fear a client might come. His first legal fee consisted of two hickory chairs.

Inevitably he interested himself in politics, but when he went to make his first speech at a neighboring village and heard himself introduced as "a brilliant young man and a rising hope of the party," he froze to his chair. In the silence the old stage driver who had brought him out reached over and whacked him.

"Get up you damned fool!"

He got up, and stayed up, fighting, for the rest of his life—lost causes a specialty.

True to his convictions about States' Rights, he helped West Virginia secede from Virginia, then found himself a southern sympathizer in a northern state and subject to a barrage of anonymous letters. He kept them as curiosities, but they did not alter his course. In 1872, an unshaken Democrat, he was surprisingly enough elected to the blackly Republican Congress of the Reconstruction Era. From his two terms in Congress he retained only the chair in which he had sat, an abiding distaste for holding office, and the knowledge that he had never compromised. Because of all the babies, his wife could not go with him to Washington, but shared his life by making fair copies of all his speeches in her flowing hand.

It was rumored that James G. Blaine had plans for John J.

Davis, but that John J. Davis would not go along. He never went along. When another West Virginian offered to support him for the Senate in return for earlier support, Grandfather sent back word that he would not play second fiddle to any man.

"Did John say that? Then we will just take his fiddle away from him." And this was done.

Personal disappointments could not dim his interest in politics, however. He found a splendid losing cause in "that plumed knight of the people," William Jennings Bryan, and in his battle against the trusts bought me a piano of unknown make to be sure of not supporting one. In 1912 he went as a delegate to the convention which nominated Woodrow Wilson. "His arm must be tired," said his daughter-in-law, "for he sat on the platform and waved his hat every time Wilson's name came up." When his candidate was nominated and later elected, it left him with little to say.

But he could always fall back, and with burning sincerity, on his fears for the state of the nation. The coals of his convictions were hot, and the smallest puff fanned them into flame. States' Rights, the sanctity of the Constitution, the freedom of the individual could always start a blaze. He liked to begin his speeches with deceptive mildness.

I am an extinct troglodyte from the remains of a past geologic age. Bodily weariness and mental lassitude subtract from the small power I might otherwise have to address you in a manner worthy of the cause.

Then he would pour it on for an hour and end with a ringing conclusion.

I charge you, if this great Republic, like a gallant ship, must drive upon the rocks, that you be on deck and with suspended breath await the shock; and should she sink beneath the destiny which has devoured other great nations of the past, that you save from the melancholy wreck our ancestral faiths, and work out yet upon this continent the problem of a free, Constitutional, and popular government. And may the God of destinies give you good issue.

This sort of thing would bring his audiences up cheering, although Grandmother would have said that his metaphors were mixed.

When I was nine, my father's friends talked of nominating him for Congress. Grandfather opposed it with force and fire. He had known the abrasive disillusionments of active politics. Young John must be saved from them. He followed him to the convention with two terse telegrams. "Refuse nomination." "Say no and stand firm."

Cautious friends put these in their pockets and did not deliver them until John W. had been unanimously acclaimed from the floor and had accepted. Once it was over, his mother made the best of it.

"Now that it is past praying for, John, I will try to be only glad of it and not think of all the drawbacks. The business may not go to the bow-wows after all. You may not escape mudballs, but you don't deserve them and they won't stick. Count on my vote and that of my friends." This last was irony and a plug for woman's suffrage. She could not resist it.

She understood her son well enough to be glad that he was taking a step into a wider world, away from the house where memory was pain, but she did not say this to him, nor he to her. It was the end of his daily life with us. From then on he came back to Clarksburg only for visits, during which all of us vied for his time. After he spent what seemed to me hours with Grandmother, she would always follow him to the door with the wistful comment, "Well, John, I haven't seen much of you *this* time."

She lived to visit him as Solicitor General. If she had been permitted to enjoy the rest of his career, she would surely have written him at each new honor, that while it was a great responsibility, with hard work he could succeed.

IV

It has seemed necessary to speak of my grandparents' early life in order to present them fully. I did not observe it, but I observed them later, and, as always between adult and child, they taught me by what they were, rather than by what they said. They had made themselves what they were by their manner of facing circumstance.

We never knew what mood Grandfather would bring home to dinner, but the chances were against its being a bright one. After a fleeting comment on his dyspepsia, he would attack his pie (the year had two seasons, rhubarb and mince), while the rest of us sat around the table waiting for our cues.

"Jefferson was right," he said darkly. "Banks are more dangerous to liberty than standing armies, and nothing should be done by any government which individuals can do for themselves."

No one commented, for fear of drawing fire.

"I tell you, Anna, all this paternalism is the dry rot of government. By and by, the government will dog the citizen at every turn, provide him with *old age pensions*, recompense him for *injuries* received through *negligence*, destroy his manhood while he is alive, and bury him when dead."

Finding herself directly addressed, Grandmother responded.

"Have you been paying your taxes, John?"

"Anna, it is no laughing matter. I don't know what we are going to do. I am getting to be a dollar-a-day man. Nothing better than a dollar-a-day man. If this goes on we will have to sell out here and let them take us to the poorhouse, lock, stock, and barrel. That is all we can do."

I had seen the grim brick poorhouse, five miles out of town on the only paved road, and the prospect appalled me. In the oppressed silence which followed this announcement, I fled howling from the table. Grandmother came to me on the porch.

"I don't think it is really going to happen, my baby. I don't think things are that bad. Grandfather is just feeling blue. He sometimes does, you know."

Of course I knew. I had only to remember what happened every Christmas to be quite sure of it. The onset of the season plunged Grandfather into gloom. "Santa Claus is very poor this year," he would say, hollowly. He would suggest that we make our lists anyway, a mere exercise in hopefulness. Then on Christmas morning we would receive everything we had suggested, and he would sit beaming in our midst.

Grandmother condemned such conduct as sentimental on the one hand and inconsistent on the other, two of her bugbears. But she rarely argued on practical points, having long since recognized her husband as a man accountable only to himself—not that he was an easy person to account to. He held himself to a code as rigid as he professed.

If I have given the impression that he was intransigent, that is correct, but with all his hair-trigger moral courage, he was not a man for physical violence. He never spanked a child, he let his horse walk all the time because he could not bear to whip it, he left his daughters to break up the really epic fights in which the big dogs engaged. It took a flock of starlings to rouse him to aggression.

One summer a plague of starlings selected our trees for their nightly roost, swooping down at dusk with a whir and a chatter, rendering the lawn untenable, murdering the evening conversation on the porch, and, final sin, waking Grandfather at dawn every morning. Streamers of cloth on the branches did not disturb them, nor did beating pans under the trees—at some risk to ourselves.

There came an evening when we waited as usual on the porch for Grandfather and saw in the distance his tall figure in the broad Panama hat and the black suit which hung loosely on his bones. This did not mean that it was time for me to run down to the gate to meet him, for he still had to pass Dr. Johnston on *his* front porch, and their discussion of the state of the nation might endure for half an hour.

But Grandfather did not stop at Dr. Johnston's. He came steadily on at his unhurried pace, proceeding up the walk between the cabbage roses and up the steps between the shrubs, whose dark red blossoms he liked to pinch and smell. *He was carrying a gun.*

Grandmother rose to the occasion. "John, what are you doing with *that?*"

"I intend to get rid of the starlings, Anna."

"You had better have dinner first. It has been ready for half an hour."

The slow dusk of that latitude was just gathering when we came out again. Grandfather put on his hat and descended the steps, while the household watched from the high gallery. He made two tries at loading the gun, raised it, fired. The birds whirred up like black leaves, then settled back. None fell. Grandfather dropped the gun and came toward us, dripping blood. He had handled it like a pistol, and the recoil had almost torn the thumb from his hand.

Grandmother, who presided over disasters with the calm of

Minerva, sent the cook flying for a basin of warm water and Aunt Em for old linen napkins and a disinfectant. Bandages were being applied when the sheriff arrived to make an arrest.

We never knew whether this official had been summoned by a neighbor who was displeased at finding himself under a hail of bird shot, or by the galvanizing sound of firing so near the jail. When he saw whom he had to arrest, a delicate situation arose, for Mr. Davis was not a man on whom the law would precipitously lay its hand. The fact remained that a gun must not be fired within the city limits.

When this was made clear, Grandfather, a just man, readily spared the sheriff further embarrassment. While holding to the principle that a man should be able to do as he pleased on his own property, if in so doing he violated some ordinance passed by thimble-witted tricksters and political imbeciles, he could not be exempted from upholding the law. As soon as the wound was dressed, still looking rather green, Grandfather went down the hill with the sheriff to turn himself in for disturbing the peace, and to pay his fine.

In his absence the gun disappeared and the incident was closed. He could not use his right hand for some weeks, and the starlings chattered more loudly than ever.

Although justly ready to pay the penalty for his own transgression, when faced by an actual sinner, Grandfather could not be harsh. When the German cook, Ida, sent word that she could not get breakfast because her back ached, he was all sympathy.

"She must have lumbago, Em. I am a martyr to it myself. Take her my Sloan's liniment and give her a good rubbing."

By the time Emma arrived on this errand of mercy, the cause of the trouble was only too clear, and the baby came before the doctor could. It was a startling occurrence in a family devoted to Victorian rectitude, but no one considered sending Ida away.

Her story of innocence and seduction was accepted, and she remained with us, unremittingly bad-tempered, until George Henry was three, teaching me with him to lift our hands and lisp our first words of German, "*Hoch der Kaiser!*" After her eventual return to Germany, financed of course by Grandfather, she wrote us for years, sending pictures of the boy, the last one in uniform.

It seems extraordinary that Grandmother, who had borne six, should also have been taken by surprise in this case, but then she lived in a world which the physical did not dominate. With access to books, paper, and pencil, she would have been happy in a cell.

Although I was only four at the time, I did gather out of the air an impression that having a baby before getting married was a great misfortune; and since I knew that God sent children, I prayed him rather earnestly for some time not to be too forehanded in such gifts to me.

The decision to take care of Ida caused no disagreement, and even no discussion between the Davises, but on minor questions of righteousness they were far apart. No disciplinarian, Grandfather left it to Grandmother to see that rules were obeyed, and the results might have surprised him if he had come out of his library long enough to see what happened.

"Sunday is not the day to play," he informed me, passing augustly by and happening to see my paper dolls spread out on the front steps. I well knew that it was not for me to argue with him, so I put the dolls away. I had endured a lifetime, seven years or so, of such Sundays, beginning with Sunday School, going on to church when legs were too short to hang over the edge of the pew, entertaining the minister for Sunday dinner whether he entertained us or not, then learning a psalm and a question in the Shorter Catechism to recite to Grandfather on his waking from his nap. This much behind me, if the day were fine he would take me for a walk to some such enlivening spot as the cemetery, which I did not mind, but stopping for half-hour conversations with friends met along the way, which I minded fiercely. In the evening all of the family returned to church except Grandmother and myself, exempted because of age, and left to play Twenty Questions with Biblical subjects.

So I put the dolls away and wandered around for a time. Then, bored beyond bearing, I asked Grandmother if I might read some fairy tales.

"That is a matter for the individual conscience to decide," she said. "If you believe it right, then it is right for you."

After a brief searching of conscience, I opted for the fairy tales. The door had been opened for me into a country where people made up their own minds, and I have lived under that wide sky ever since.

It was Grandmother's country, of course. She had no intention of living anywhere else, and she wished to have her children there with her. She never censored my reading, remembering that she herself had been told not to read Byron, "the only book I ever read behind a door," but she reserved the right to tell me that my taste was poor.

"Reading that trash again?" she inquired, seeing me with a popular magazine. No answer was required, and none was made. "Well," she continued, "I hope you will marry a poor man, for you will never amount to anything if you don't." After which pungent comment she went briskly on about her business.

I must allow her one exception to this excellent rule of non-interference. *The Klansmen*, with its sex crimes and overtones of racial prejudice, was too much for her in my childish hands. I read it behind the bookcase in the library bay window—and missed the point entirely.

In great matters of doctrine as well as in small observances she held to her principle of independent thinking. I came back from boarding school and told her with some trepidation that I no longer believed in the virgin birth of Jesus.

"I haven't believed in that since I was able to think for myself," she told me, "and it does not make a bit of difference. Christ's place in history and the value of his teaching are not dependent on a physical miracle."

When I pressed her further on the nature of the deity, she shook her head, looking at me with affectionate tolerance. "The wisest minds have not been able to answer these questions. I doubt that you will. Just let it go for a time."

Tolerance could not, however, be extended to draw a hazy line between right and wrong. The rules were clear, although transgressors could take comfort in the fact that forgiveness could be obtained. This was proved for me when I told my Great Lie.

Playing alone as was all too usual, I saw a group of Italian miners go up the hill to the mine behind it. They waved at the *bambina* as they passed.

Too much solitude had overstimulated my imagination. I waved back, then thoughtfully made my way to the kitchen and told the cook that they had tried to kidnap me and had chased me all the way to the house.

It was at the time of a Black Hand and Mafia scare in the town. Murders had been committed by members of these organizations, and later seven of them were hanged. Some of this may have filtered down to me in table talk. My "experience" was widely reported, and anxious mothers all over town added the fear of kidnaping to their other worries. I was not allowed to play near the street or out of sight for the rest of the summer.

I did not feel gratified at the commotion. In fact, I hardly noticed it. I had invented an interesting story with obvious audience appeal, and that was enough. It passed out of my mind. A year later, two years later (who can measure the days of childhood?), the voice of conscience suddenly spoke to me in the orchard, saying, "*You lied.*"

My training had not been neglected. I knew that a lie was one of the worst of sins, striking at the root of human intercourse. A man had to fight anyone who accused him of it; a woman dropped that person from her acquaintance. However, when you sinned there were three things you must do. You must repent. You must ask God for forgiveness. You must try to make reparation here on earth.

I repented. On my knees, in tears, among the long orchard grasses, I asked God for forgiveness. Still weeping, I went to the front gate to wait for Grandmother and Aunt Emma, who were paying calls.

This custom involved some ceremony. It took place between three and five in the afternoon and called for proper regalia —a fresh white ruching around the boned collar, the best turban with the flowered crown, the silver card case held in the black kid glove. If the friend were at home, half an hour was the permissible limit of stay, or if engaged in homely pursuits such as putting up fruit or washing her hair, she might without offense send word that she was out. Grandmother found the whole process so tedious that she forced herself to it only once or twice a year.

Now, returning with the happy consciousness of having it behind her, she was met by a sobbing child who hurled herself into her arms.

"Why, precious baby, what has happened?"

I was crying too bitterly to get it out. She had to ask several times.

"You know what I told you about the Italians chasing me?"

Her arms tightened. "Yes. Of course. Has it happened again?"

"It never did happen. It wasn't *so!*"

She needed a moment's silence to adjust to this.

"They didn't chase you at all?"

"No. They just waved at me. That's all they did."

"Well . . . well . . ." She took a deep breath. "I am very glad to know it. I have repeated that story to all my friends, and now I can tell them it is not so, and people will not be blamed for what they did not do. You have done right to set it straight. Don't cry any more."

Anna Davis was not in any sense a woman who liked to tie her children to her. The more boldly they went out into the world, the better she was pleased, and never did she write a word to any of them which might pull them back. They were her lifework, and they must repay her by standing on their own feet. It was her husband from whom she could not bear to be separated.

Once she cut short a visit to her daughter Lillie and hurried home. "To tell the truth, Em, Mr. Preston was so polite to me all the time, I was spoiling for a fight."

In spite of their differences of temperament and opinion, Grandfather felt the same about her.

"Home would be a lonesome place without you," he wrote when she went to Baltimore to see a doctor, "so it will pay me to see that you are taken care of."

One summer my father took her and Aunt Emma to Europe. Grandfather declined to go, preferring to journey by means of travel books in the comfort of his armchair. His library was his ship and his castle. There his desk stood in the middle of the room, piled high with papers except for the island occupied by the oil lamp. He needed only one Morris chair by the window and one by the desk, and permitted no more in his sanctuary. Here he spent his quiet evenings and his Sunday afternoons, and here he had all that he required without the vanity and disturbance of travel.

When our natural protectors departed, Aunt Lillie and Aunt

Nan came to take care of Grandfather and me—no fair exchange. On the day of return, Aunt Nan, whose exuberance never knew the words "too much," hung flags and paper banners everywhere. At the gate, WELCOME HOME; on the walk, in imitation of a neighbor, "We Will Never Leave Her Go Again"; on the steps, "Hail to the Lady who rode on a Pony from the Gap of Dunloe to the Lake of Killarney" (oh dear); and climactically over the front door, HAIL TO THE QUEEN.

Grandfather came through the hall and saw me watching the arrangements. "She will be here soon," he said. (Not your Father, not Em.) "She will be here soon." Before my astonished eyes he held out the skirts of his black frock coat and danced an Irish jig.

The inevitable separation came at last. Through the months of his last illness she rarely left his room. With the futile young belief that something could be done to spare her, I remonstrated that she must take care of herself. She answered with a sad finality.

"Ah, my girlie, if someone would tell me that your Grandfather will get well, I should be all right. But nobody is going to tell me that."

After his death I heard her crying aloud, like an animal in pain. It was as shocking as if the hill behind our house had crumbled. "Half of me is gone," she said.

She followed him within a year and not all the doctors at Johns Hopkins could stop her, but she did not take the ultimate journey until she had installed two more bathrooms, electricity throughout the house, eliminated the last coal fire, and sold the cows, horses, and chickens which Grandfather had insisted on keeping in the center of town.

V

The mosaic of life in Clarksburg would not be complete without space for the aunts, nor would it be fair not to let them be heard, for each in her own way was unique, and gave to life fully of her special gifts. I was fifteen when Grandfather died, sixteen when I lost Grandmother, but the aunts stayed with me until a few years ago.

First above all came my lovable, indispensable Aunt Emma. Hers were the hands which tended all of us. If she had been willing to subside into the role, she could have become the classic spinster, the Martha in a family of dedicated Marys, the Universal Aunt.

But Miss Emma was a woman of unusual interests. At one time she had three murderers staying with her. This was of course after her parents had died, when she was alone in the house. Nor had she acquired such a group of friends overnight. She had collected them gradually.

To reflect that Lillie and Nan married while Emma did not, is to lose faith in the judgment of the male sex. Lill lived by preference on white bread and cold milk; Nan would not sew on a button without an audience; Emma, as plump and matronly as her sisters were sparse, enjoyed all the things which made domestic life comfortable and happy.

In my childhood she buttoned me up. To my ferris waist she buttoned the drawers and the suspenders for the long black stockings, also the flannel petticoat. Over this structure she buttoned a starched slip with many pearl buttons down the back, and a ruffled dress with the same. She buttoned the high shoes with a buttonhook, as well as the leggings and the kid gloves. No wonder Grandmother's button box could take a scholar through 12 x 12. Day after day, and several times a day, Aunt Emma prepared this little artifact to face the world, and did it always with love and no complaints. She was my slave. While she made my clothes I made her play at being all the animals in *The Jungle Book*, dialogue by me. I was Mowgli of course. Aunt Nan would have taken the game away from me and made it better, but not mine. Besides, she would have had to have the lead.

What some man lost, Em's family gained. As the phrase went, before the idea became abhorrent, she took care of her parents. If cook or maid left, Em pitched in; if the outside man was too hungover to milk the cows on Sunday morning, Em hunted a substitute in the shacks along the river. She presided over all domestic rites, from the autumnal apple butter—stirred all day with a long wooden paddle over a campfire in the back yard —to the spring cleaning. With her head tied in a towel she climbed ladders to dust the myriad books, she washed the long lace curtains and fastened them on stretchers to dry in the sun, she took up the carpets and beat them on the line. To me, spring cleaning was a fascinating break in routine when that which was high could be brought low and handled, but conceivably to her it had less allure.

Like the rest of the family, I imposed on her shamelessly, and she bore it with a cheerful heart. When I was quite small, the doctor ordered her to Atlantic City for a rest. With her usual attention to my feelings, she planned to leave late at night so as not to upset me with good-bys, but I was not to be fooled. I turned on her as she put me to bed.

"You wouldn't leave your baby, would you, Amma?"

"What makes you ask that?"

"You wouldn't *leave* her, would you?"

"Not for long."

"Who would keep care of me if you went away?"

"Lots of people." She enumerated them.

"Amma, you are the bestest one to keep care of me. You let the others go and you stay here."

More of this, and my poor beleaguered darling went downstairs in despair. "Mother, it's all off. I can't go."

"Nonsense," said Grandmother, no friend to sentimentality. "She will have forgotten you by noon tomorrow."

Little wretch that I was, I did just that.

She gave to us all so lightheartedly and freely that we had no compunction about taking from her. It seemed to be what she was *meant* to do. "I have never had a choice in life," she told me. "For me it has always been 'This is the way. Walk thou therein.' "

She walked with a firm step, but it is not true that she made no choices. She made many.

Her buoyant nature was not a gift from heaven, but her own creation. In her twenties she labored for months under a severe depression, life slipping by, the future no more than the past. She told no one about it, not even her mother. Fighting it alone, she conquered it for all time. In her forties she helped a young man with a similar problem, fell in love with him, although she knew that love for her had come too late. She transmuted her feeling into a friendship which lasted the rest of her life.

Her need for giving soon outran the family circle. She chose to broaden her life not by giving up any duties but by adding new ones. While Aunt Nan's husband was minister of our (or Grandfather's) church, the two sisters founded the Mission Sunday School.

Out on the Milford Road a family called McAtee lived in

unholy poverty and accumulated around them a group as racy as themselves. The pompous, patriarchal McAtee was rumored to have been a Virginia gentleman brought down by drink. His wife, Old Nance, was purely mountain woman. After she and my aunts became friends, she would sit by the hour on our porch, intoning in a nasal voice the English ballads preserved and distorted in her native hills and hollows. Aunt Nan had several of them published by the American Folklore Society. Although surrounded all her life by cabins and shacks, Old Nance sang of "castels" (confusing them with caskets), of great halls, marble stones, lace-bordered winding sheets, as if they had been the natural materials of her fancy.

Mamie, the feeble-minded and unmarried daughter, was the town drab and beggar woman, whom the little boys called Sweet Potato because once she had stolen some. When the last of her several unidentified babies died, "after eating her salt pork and cabbage as good as anybody," my aunts decided that Mamie needed help.

One thing led to another, and soon the McAtees and friends, who had until then resisted authority with violence, were coming to the church every Sunday afternoon to learn something about deportment, godliness, and its neighbor, cleanliness. They kept coming until the first set of children were naming their children Emma and Nan. Within reasonable limits, they made an effort to conform.

"Mith Emma," little Annie Bunnell lisped each Sunday, "I've quit cuthing."

"That's fine, Annie. You shouldn't cuss. When did you stop?"

"Yithtiddy."

It is not recorded that any of the McAtees really quit cussing. They continued to get drunk, break the peace, and even appropriate the property of others. But they came to have a high regard for their more conforming friends, and on at least one day a week, shining with soft soap and serious purpose, they behaved as well as anybody.

When one of the McAtee boys was put in jail, a not too unusual circumstance, his mother came complaining to Miss Emma, and Miss Emma went down to the jail with a jar of soup to see what she could do for him. The conditions she found landed her eventually in the prison work which she kept up for twenty-five years.

The sheriff, allotted thirty cents a day to feed each prisoner, managed with weak soup and beans to spend only six. Young offenders and hardened criminals occupied the cell blocks together and entertained themselves by shouting obscenities at the women's ward across the court, getting back as good as they sent. The sick lay in their bunks until they recovered without care, and although a man might be held for six months merely awaiting trial, there was nothing, absolutely nothing, for anyone to do.

Miss Emma went to work with baskets of food, complaints to officials, lessons in reading and writing for any who expressed interest, books, and group singing on Sunday afternoons. Sitting on our front porch we could hear them clearly: "Tell Mother I'll be There," "Shall we Gather at the River?" and the prime favorite, "O for the Wings of a Dove." Musically the performance left something to be wished, but it was better than cursing.

Our volunteer, herself surprised, had no method beyond taking a warm personal interest in each prisoner, which soon entailed finding jobs for those who were released, or visiting those who graduated to the state penitentiary in Moundsville. In the penitentiary she made warm friends, only one of whom was a warden. She became so well known that she was sent as a delegate to a prison conference in London, but her approach remained always personal rather than organizational.

She saw her new associates, most of whom were half her age, as boys in trouble who had no one to help them. They needed a friend, and she knew how to be one.

She was horrified at the brutality of the punishment: the beatings, the weeks in solitary or dark cells, the fire hose stuck in a prisoner's mouth and turned on until his stomach burst. The men were at the mercy of the warden, and the warden was a political appointee. She watched prison administrations come and go, some enlightened, and some not.

Above all, she felt the loneliness of the convicts. To be cut off from life, encased in nothingness, unloved and unloving, is to experience hell. She had more love to give than her family could use. She spent it on those who could not find it elsewhere.

The prison authorities, at first suspicious, soon allowed her to visit anyone she pleased, and suggested others. Then they began to parole offenders in her case. That is how she acquired her three murderers.

Willie C. was a nice boy (they were all nice boys), who had made the mistake of shooting an uncle, called Devil Anse, of the Governor of West Virginia. It was in self-defense, of course, but Miss Davis had to work her way through three successive governors before she found one with the courage to pardon Willie.

There he sat on the back porch, wearing a kitchen apron and shelling beans for her, while she cast about to find a place where he might recommence his life. It was thought that his native mountains might not be healthy for him, feuding being what it is. She found an opening in Ohio for Willie.

Jim was a Negro and a good cook, who in time got married in our back parlor, wearing one of Grandfather's top hats and his frock coat. Jim had had trouble with his former mate.

"I never meant to kill her, Miss Davis. Just scratch her throat a little with a razor."

"Have you told your fiancée what happened to your first wife?"

"Lord no, Miss Davis. What she don't know won't hurt her."

Lee North had committed his murder at sixteen. Up in the mountains he and another boy raised a calf, sold it at a fair, quarreled on the way home over how to divide the five dollars. Unfortunately they had a jug of whisky, and Lee had a gun. When he saw that his friend was dying, he stayed by him, tried to staunch the wound, brought water from the brook in his hat, made every effort to undo what had been done.

When Chester died, Lee ran away. He hopped freights, visited cities, walked crowded streets, learned evil from hoboes, worked at what he could find, lived as he might. Through it all the mountains called to him, called him wherever he was.

One day he heard a bird sing in a city square. He knew the notes. Closing his eyes he could see it flying against an open sky. He could bear his exile no longer. Knowing the danger, knowing what he faced, caring for nothing but to see his wild green hills again, he went back, stood trial, and was sentenced to prison for life.

Now under his feet he trod stones instead of earth. Instead of looking across the rolling valleys his barred window showed him a dusty courtyard. He had lost, as he thought forever, air, silence, freedom, beauty, and the companionship of growing things. When my Aunt Emma met him he had been sixteen years in prison, a man of thirty-three, potentially strong, with hair still reddish-brown, but a face deeply grooved by a concentrated suffering, a singlehearted woe.

Boyhood aborted, manhood had come in bitterness. Since he could neither read nor write he could only think, and his thoughts traveled perpetually their rutted road.

One night as he lay on his bunk the light in the corridor went out from the master switch. "Some day," he told himself, "your life will go out like that light." Suddenly he was swept by the feeling of wasted, passing, irrecoverable time. He got up, fell on his knees by the cot, made his first effort at a prayer.

"Oh God, help me to have some sense."

The prayer strengthened him. Next day he asked for a Bible and laboriously began to teach himself to read, comparing the passages with what he heard in the prison chapel. He heard of Miss Davis, the woman who came to see people, and asked to meet her. She arranged correspondence courses for him. He proved to have a mind as thirsty and receptive as a dry run in summer.

He worked at learning in every free moment. After several years, Aunt Emma persuaded Berea College in Kentucky to say that he might come there for special courses if he were freed. With a definite plan to present, she was able to persuade the governor to pardon him.

On his way to the college he passed through Clarksburg, walking the world like a man who has forgotten what to expect of it. He sat beside Miss Emma in the porch swing, pressing his broad rough hands together until the knuckles showed white. He could think of only one thing to say, over and over.

"I owe you my life, Miss Davis. I owe you my *life*."

He did so well at Berea that the Presbyterian church appointed him a lay missionary in the mountains which he never voluntarily left for long. A gang of toughs tried to run him out of his first post, and well-wishers advised him not to hold a meeting. When he went ahead in spite of threats, the gang lounged in and sat down, grinning. As he preached, they began to shuffle their feet, softly at first, then more loudly, over the bare boards. Then they whistled. Then they knocked with their knuckles on the benches. Lee paused in his discourse, drew a pistol from his pocket, laid it across the open Bible in front of him. Over it he looked at his hecklers, man by man.

"I've shot one man. I hope I never have to shoot another."

The meeting proceeded in a decent silence. "God made this old world a lovely place," he told them. "What thorns there is, we grow them ourselfs."

Miss Davis went to his wedding in a glen so remote that she rode the last ten miles on a white mule. Although his prison life had affected his health, for three years his letters were full of delight in his "sweet wife," his two baby boys.

"I reckon I feel like old Lazarus when Jesus called him back to this world. My lungs don't let me preach much, but if there was as many Holy Rollers as there is sparks in hell, still I would continue to serve God in my own way. The baby is awful cute, and so is Della, ha-ha!"

But even the mountains, remote, simple, wild, were not saved from the influenza epidemic of 1919. When it struck, the mountain people had built up no resistance. Within three days Lee watched Della die, and six of her family. Ill himself, staggering with weakness, Lee alone made Della's coffin, dressed her, dug her grave. No neighbor dared to come and help. The youngest baby died soon after. "Bad feeding," he reported laconically.

There was no one to whom he could cry his sorrows except Miss Davis. "Here comes Job again. 'Though He slay me, yet will I trust Him.' "

His native strength asserted itself, he rallied, and began anew on what was always to be a problem for him, the hard business of making a living. His lungs, weakened by sixteen years of prison, would not allow him to preach, nor to work long in the mines. He tried road work, farming, anything. "I don't know myself how I manage, but I do."

Miss Davis saw a way to be of practical assistance. She took his two-year-old son and kept him for six months.

Somehow Lee survived and rebuilt his life. In time he married again and at last achieved his goal, "a nice family, a patch of land, and the house that Lee built."

"I will tell you my history. I was born twice in the grand state of West Virginia. Born of the flesh in Wyoming county, born of the spirit in a prison cell, and a blacker heart never found the regenerating power of Jesus than the one I laid before him."

Thirty years after the prison gates had opened, and shortly before Aunt Emma's death, he sent her a birthday letter.

My dear dear Miss Davis,

I am sure you do not know what it means to me to write a letter to you. Have you ever stopped to think that you was first to speak words of kindness, first to plant in my heart a desire for high and noble things—first to make me feel that someone cared—first to give me a chance to live at all.

Did not the rest of mankind push me away as undesirable, confine me in a living hell, and steal the best years of my life? I am not bitter at the world. They did me wrong because they did not understand. It was you only that dared and give me the only chance I ever had in life. If I loved you only for what you did for me it might be easy to write, but I love you for what you are, and that makes writing a different thing. Mental and social mountains may stand between persons and the things they love, but mountains cannot and does not in any sense hinder love.

Do not mistake me. This is no love letter. It is only love looking backward across the mountains that hindered. Bless your good and unselfish heart, you have meant everything to me.

. . . When I am through checking after Fosdick, I will then let you know what I think about the book.

Many were the life histories which unfolded themselves to Aunt Emma, and varied the friends who came to visit her. Since she could not afford a maid when she first lived alone, she called the servant's room her "prophet's chamber," and gave it to anyone who needed a bed for a night or two. They arrived at all seasons. Sometimes, with an acquired caution about giving their names, they merely sat on the front porch until she came out, confident that they would not be turned away.

About this time she abandoned Grandfather's nightly ceremony of locking up. In summer the front door might stand open all night, letting the house cool. "It would take a mighty mean man to rob me. I have too many friends in the business." For the record, she was never robbed.

An Italian baron gave her language lessons; a stranger of good family who had kited a check stayed for a month; Arturo Suarez decorated his communications with swirling flowers, flags, and flying angels drawn in crayon.

My dear and loveably friend,

I am almost too happy to tell it. Yes! Sunshine everywhere I look upon. I meant around and in a side of poor me. Do you know why? Sure you do. But in case you have forgotten it already, a thing that never happens with your beloved person, I am too happy beccausse I can now see in front of me the wonderful day when *I shall go free once more and to stay free too. Oh!*

I thank you most warmly for been happy with me. I love you more than like a son could love his mother.

Joseph Campetelli, "her everly Italian son," had an even fiercer battle with the language, but his meaning came through.

Gentless Miss Davis,

Its one week since I wrote you and you did not answer yet. I want what is the matter. I hope this letter find you happy. Please answer me soon because I do not know what to think about.

How much words I said the affection and loved but are not capable writings in English. The name mother it pronunciation with emphasis and gaiety the heart. I cannot recompense you. Only the good God recompense you and entirely family for the good and excellent heart that you have. To thank the heart.

Benton Amos was taken away from his mother at four by some neighbors who had temporary care of him. When she found him again, he was dying of tuberculosis in the penitentiary. Although the warden recommended that he be paroled in her care, the disease moved more swiftly than the law. By the time his mother could scrape together the money to visit him, she arrived on the day before he died. When it was over the warden sent Aunt Emma her letters.

I have shed enough tears over you to make a river from here to Moundsville since you was taken away from me. I was so glad to hear from you, but oh so sorry to know where you was at. The two boys I raised myself never was arrested and in no trouble at all, and I think I could have raised you the same way. If they would let me stay in that lonesome place and release you, I would take your place so you could be out in the fresh air.

May God forgive you and the governor pardon you and send you home to me is my prayer.

P.S. Mr. Warden, please be good to my baby.

Harry Howard found a puppy when he was working on the road, and hid her in his cell until he had taught her some tricks. Then he showed her off to the warden and got permission to keep her.

My little dog Bridget who is sitting in front of the cell door is crying. Poor little dogie, she saw a little boy and a little dog on the street playing and she seems to take it very much to heart. I am sure she realizes that she is also in prison.

Your adopted friend,
Harry Howard.

Out of prison bitterness, someone poisoned Harry's little companion. "I know now that I truly love God, Miss Davis, for I know who was the man who poisoned Bridget, and I did not kill him."

Roy King had, and relished, the reputation of being "the worst man in the pen." Punishment cells and beatings could not tame him. He asked permission to write to Miss Davis. This was available to anyone, but since each prisoner could send out only two letters a month, those who had friends or family did not waste their scanty privilege on her, and her mail was not overloaded. King smuggled out an offensive letter. She replied briefly that he was not to write again.

On her next trip to the prison, he asked to be allowed to see her and apologize. The warden advised against it. She said that she would see him, because a man should always be given a chance to set his conscience straight.

It had become the custom for her to talk with each man alone in a small room with the door locked on the outside. The warden said that he would put a guard in the room when she talked with King. "This is a dangerous man. I wouldn't want to be shut up with him myself alone, unless I had a gun." Miss Davis said that she would see him in the same way that she saw the others.

The guard who brought King in went out reluctantly. As she stood up to greet him, she heard the key turn in the lock. It must have been a strange encounter, the small plump spinster, firm on her tiny feet, the brawny man, red-faced as a schoolboy, rubbing his hands together and repeating, "I'm sorry I wrote you that letter, Miss Davis. I'm sorry I wrote you that letter."

"You made a mistake, Roy King. We will say no more about it. Sit down and let's talk."

The interview proceeded normally, but he never became one of her close friends. In due course he was released, and she heard no more of him. Years later she was on a train in a remote part of West Virginia, when a man came up to her seat.

They were alone in the car, and she saw a gun in a holster on his hip.

"Do you remember me, Miss Davis?"

"Of course I remember you, Roy King."

"I just want to tell you, Miss Davis, I'm going straight. I'm a deputy sheriff now. You did it, Miss Davis. It was your courage and the way you stood up to me."

The train stopped at a mountain station and King got off. Their paths never crossed again.

Aunt Emma always declined to write her prison stories, the poignant dramatic histories of men who had lost their way, been shut off and forgotten, yet retained their individualities however narrowly repressed, sprouting like grass between stones. As she told of them her gray eyes kindled with emotion, her cheeks flushed pink.

Grandfather was alive when Aunt Emma started "going to the pen," but needless to say he had died before she began bringing the graduates home. Grandmother, with her inexhaustible interest in every phase of life, approved. The sisters deplored, but the dire consequences they predicted never came to pass.

Once launched into outside interests, Aunt Emma could not stop. With friends she organized the Clarksburg Public Library in someone's double parlor and saw it grow into a thriving institution with a building of its own. She was one of those who moved the city fathers to pay a public nurse, and she interested herself in civic reform.

"I wonder what you would have thought of me standing in the courthouse basement all day Tuesday during the town election. I thought of Papa all the time and knew he would have had me arrested as a lunatic."

During the First World War she was chairman of the Red

Cross in our county, and then became director of relief. This brought her new friends with new problems.

"What do you mean, Guiseppe, by having another baby when there are thirteen of you on relief already?"

"I didn't did it, Miss Davis. Jesus Christ did it."

The McAtee family never let go of her. "I shall ask Nance about it the next time she comes up to borrow money, which she is due to do before long. She says she likes to borrow from rich folks."

Selby McAtee, the only one of the family who kept out of jail and even held a steady job, was drafted, and Nance brought her trouble to the usual place.

"Miss Emma, I want you should write the govmint for me. They tell me there's two of them so one is there if the other feller goes away. You tell him to let Selby stay home because I need him. Honest I do. I don't hold with sending our boys acrost the river to fight them people anyways. We had ought to line up on this bank and shoot them as they climb out of the water."

Miss Emma persuaded her to accept the inevitable, then went with her to see Selby off. The whole clan were at the station, washed, tearful, smelling only faintly of drink. Selby leaned out of the train window and waved his hat.

"I'm a-goin to git him!"

"Git who?" the McAtees shouted.

"The feller they're sendin me after!"

But although Aunt Emma took care of so many people, we could not complain that she neglected us. If a sister fell ill, Em went to nurse her. When I had an operation in London, she came to me there. She arrived at the nursing home so early in the morning that the doorman would not admit her.

"But I *must* get in. My child is being operated on."

"What is your name, madam?"

"Miss Davis."

She always laughed when she remembered his shocked expression. If he had known her he would not have wasted time in trying to stop her.

We remember her laughter. It is hard to remember that she was handicapped. She grew very deaf, always maintaining that she heard very well unless people mumbled, or, conversely, that being deaf kept her from being bored by a lot of nonsense which she did not wish to hear. "I can't understand the New York lingo," she complained. In Clarksburg everyone shouted "GOOD MORNING MISS EMMA," when they met her. In New York they did not know enough to do that. I discovered that I could make her hear me all over the house if I squeaked like a bat, for she was less deaf in the upper register.

When she was sixty-three she lost her right arm in an automobile accident. The car overturned and the arm was cut off by the cable edging the road. Before she could be lifted out, she directed the putting on of a tourniquet. In the ambulance she said calmly, "I'll be gone before night," then, reflecting that this might not be so, "I'll never work again." By this she referred to the sewing and embroidery which had become her hobby after she gave up painting.

As soon as she came out of the hospital, she made a hooked rug on a frame, punching the wool through with a left hand which had been broken at the wrist and set crooked some years before. As she trained this hand, she worked as well as ever, winning prizes with designs she had drawn herself. She typed, she gardened, she cut her hair short to make it easier to handle, she managed her food with a "Nelson knife." She wore capes on all her dresses, and with them floating behind her as she swung along, she looked like a ship under sail. My father, who by this time took care of all family emergencies in his own way, provided her with a maid-companion, but the worst thing kind Louise Harrison could do was to offer help which Aunt Emma did not think she needed.

All this had a purpose. I had been the driver of the car. When she found that she was not going to die she said, "I've got to carry on for Julia's sake." She did so, for fifteen active years.

She never spoke of her difficulties. Her undaunted passage through life gave her a beautiful face. In her girlhood, gray-green eyes, dark hair, and an uptilted nose were not in style, but after her hair turned white, her cheeks pink, and the glow of her spirit shone through, she was called lovely. It pleased her, but she was not convinced. She enjoyed bright colors and pretty clothes, however, and if she had a vanity it was for her neat ankles and little feet.

The older she grew the less she feared—not criminals, not public opinion, not handicaps, not death. "It's lucky I wasn't a man," she said. "I'd have been a rip."

Her last years were her best; loneliness overcome and put to good account, handicaps surmounted, friends everywhere. Under her management a fresh breeze blew through the old house. Many shared it with her at one time or another, and her interest in their lives enriched her own.

The automobile accident brought her the unusual experience of reading her own obituary in a local paper. "A noble West Virginia woman," it called her. On her tombstone my father had five words engraved: "Of the best and bravest."

VI

No one could have called Aunt Nan either notably brave or domestically useful, but she had her own unforgettable influence on my childhood, and she too made her life both interesting and memorable. I knew her first as the voice which told the fairy tales, which dramatized the most ordinary events, which lured us like the Pied Piper's flute into wild flights of imagination.

She made a splendid playmate, not because she was kinder and more patient than a child—she was not—but because she could invent more exciting pastimes. A child herself forever, she saw the world as she wished to see it. For her each commonplace object had a symbolic meaning, and since children would follow her into that cosmos where nothing was merely what it seemed, she preferred them to adults, whose feet were usually stuck in the cement of reality.

In memory I can see her more vividly than most of the rest, for she and Grandfather had a pictorial quality which the others lacked. She is coming down the long hall, a slender woman in pink mull, shirred at the waist, her dark eyes flashing under a great hat loaded with roses—giving me a first intimation of what clothes do for a woman's looks. She is getting ready for bed in layers of flannel, for she was always chilly, brushing and braiding her heavy hair, white since her twenties. She is leading a group of children in a wild rout through the two parlors until she drops to the floor with them in a circle around her. I have no pictures of her doing any sort of domestic work.

With her animation and her flair, she managed to be beautiful in spite of a curvature of the spine, which with her habitual exaggeration she called a hump. In her youth an effort was made to correct it by hanging her in a harness in the stair well and drawing her up until her toes barely touched the floor. She described this in bloodcurdling terms, a child screaming in agony while a fiendish uncle laughed as he turned a winch on the top floor. Knowing her capacity for protest, I doubt if he did it more than once against her will. In any case, the results were not what had been hoped. It in no wise hindered her gift for dramatic entrances and exits, and when on stage she made unfailingly for the center.

"I am a changeling!" she would cry, her eyes wild and brilliant. "I know I am a changeling! The trolls came out of that hill one night when the north wind blew, and put me in the cradle. Mother did not know when they took the other Nancy away. How else would the child of two such blue-eyed people have brown eyes?"

Changeling or not, she was Grandfather's daughter, with his fluency, his dramatics, his fierce emotionalism, his unreasonable fears, and she treated him with a lese majesty no one else dared. "Dear Pop," she wrote him, and signed it, "Your damn fool."

Although she sincerely tried to play her part as an adult, the mask kept slipping. The symbol of the changeling expressed her inner bewilderment at what life required of her.

This barely captured Tinkerbell married Hilary Goode Richardson, a mystic and a saint. Not a benign, beaming-God's-love-to-all-creatures saint, but a desert-wandering, ascetic spiritual adventurer. If in fact he never saw a desert, that was only because he married Nan. They pulled in unequal harness for nearly fifty years, with rare devotion, and considerable mouthing at the bit.

He claimed that he had entered the theological seminary

only because it was the best way to acquire a background for his true vocation, archaeology. His black eyes gleaming with the hope of shocking his auditor, he liked to repeat the advice of his favorite professor.

"Richardson, you will soon be ordained, and will take charge of a church, an awe-inspiring responsibility. You will start preaching to your congregation about all that you have learned here, and after a few weeks, you will have told them all you know. Appalled, you will face an infinity of Sundays on each of which you must produce a discourse, or perhaps two. Do not give way to panic. When you have told all you know, you can begin to preach about that which you do *not* know, and, my boy, the field is unlimited."

Limitless indeed Hilary Richardson found the possibilities of learning, and hotly he pursued the truth which he hoped might be found in knowledge. His restless search for the ultimate did not take him down an easy road. He was sustained in his quest only by a burning faith in the God whom he sought.

His first step on the long road was to leave the Episcopal church of his Virginia childhood for the more rigorous Presbyterian denomination. He accepted the call to Clarksburg because an archaeological expedition in which he had enrolled was postponed for lack of funds. There he met Nan, and that was the end of the Near East.

His sermons were too thoughtful for his congregation, and he was soon, and justly, suspected of heretical ideas. Another minister who found him reading Darwin and Huxley took him to task for wasting his time on subversive stuff.

"Have you read these authors?"

"Certainly not."

"Then don't waste my time discussing something you know nothing about."

He was so abrupt only with those who tried to push him

against his beliefs, but these unfortunately came to include the governing bodies of the Presbyterian church.

On the human side, his flock could not complain of him as a pastor. He quivered with sympathy for those in distress, children swarmed to him, and when one of the prostitutes in town was dying, only he among the clergy went in and out to see her with no fear for the possible scandal.

One stormy night he was praying for guidance as to how to raise one hundred dollars needed for an ill parishioner, when a knock came at his door. Opening it he found a man whom he did not recognize.

"You were kind to me years ago, Mr. Richardson. I happened to be in town between trains, and I had a sudden impulse to come and give you something for your work." The stranger handed him one hundred dollars and went away.

Uncle Dick used to tell this story with amazement, too much a mystic to accept it as sheer coincidence, too much a skeptic to attach to it any supernatural significance.

When I first knew this improbable combination, the husband who cared for nothing but the bare bones of truth, the wife who gave it small room and no affection, they lived in the little gray manse a block from our house. My mother's death had frightened Aunt Nan out of having children, and they attached themselves to me. I was sure of superior entertainment when I went there, and I climbed the hill as often as possible.

Uncle Dick would lunge out of his study, his craggy face beaming with pleasure, collapse into a chair like an elongated marionette whose strings have been dropped, and do one of his tricks for my amusement. He could wiggle his ears, which stood out widely, and he could break an egg on his head without getting it into his shock of black hair. His burning, deep-set eyes, his wide mobile mouth could express the whole range of human emotion, and always with intensity. After a spellbinding performance, he would go back to work, while Nan Dit and I played all over the house.

"Don't go near the tool shed, Julia. The Covenanters meet there tonight, and no one may enter it who has not taken the oath."

The Covenanters were her boys' club, soon so popular that it expanded beyond the limits of the church and even included the son of the Chinese laundryman. He seemed an unusual heir to the Covenanting tradition of the Scottish highlands, but after he went back to Shanghai he wrote her as a son for the rest of his life.

I never caught her doing routine chores. Early in her married life an awful sense of duty led her to darn one of Hilary's socks. It was her story that he cut the darn out and threw the sock away, declaring that he had not married her to have her do that sort of work. It is my belief that she made such a production of it that he had no alternative.

I might find her planning a party, and her parties were notable. I was allowed to be Alice at a Mad Hatter's dinner, where all the adult guests, in costume, leapt up between each course and changed seats to cries of "Faster! Faster!" The Dormouse, asleep of course, had to be moved forcibly each time. The Ladies Aid Society were once served their dinner by a fat Negress in calico who slopped soup and broke dishes and proved to be the dominie himself, well padded and in black face.

"I hate dull people," Nan said. "I could sandbag my best friend to create action."

With her friends, with the gift for handling groups of young people which was her greatest talent, with the closeness to "home" and family, Aunt Nan could have been happy always as the minister's wife in Clarksburg. It was not to be. The yeast of conscience began to work in Uncle Dick. Nan liked to claim psychic experiences, to say that she felt things in her bones. We did not take her premonitions as seriously as she wished. Outstandingly, her bones neglected to warn her that Uncle Dick would carry her into exile.

She had been the pretty, the petted, the baby sister, and she felt secure only at "home," a word she never used for any other domicile. After the Richardsons left Clarksburg she came back for a long visit each year, although she could not induce him to stay for more than a week. If any spirit can return to haunt that ruined site, it will be hers.

But Uncle Dick resigned his ministry in Clarksburg because he wished to go more deeply into the sources of his religion. He moved to Baltimore and studied Semitic languages at Johns Hopkins. He had some savings, they lived frugally, and he augmented their income by preaching as supply in a church outside the city. Nan tried to make the best of it.

"Now I can get down to work, Mother. I always have to talk to you a little first, or nothing seems any good. Lill's visit was strenuous, but kept me from wandering around out home, and when I am not homesick I can eat. That tremulousness in my muscles is much better, my throat, however, has never let up on that choking sensation, and when they sing in that big church I feel as if all that noise was sucking the wind out of me.

"Two of the professors came in to supper. I like having congenial people with brains gathered in my drawing room. N.B. If you have room to draw your breath, isn't it a drawing room?"

Even this moderate tranquillity could not last. Hilary's doubts grew with his studies, and he ceased to believe in the orthodox teachings of his church. Some of his colleagues advised him to keep quiet about it, not to make trouble for himself, to realize that other ministers also had uncertainties, but thought it best not to express them.

This was not Hilary's way. He wrote to his synod, was called before them, professed his heresies, and was read out of the church.

The action rapidly made itself felt in a material sense, for preaching had been his only source of income; but both he and Nan were too proud to let their families know how stringent the situation became. He published articles, more distinguished than remunerative, in such magazines as the *Harvard Theological Review* and the *American Journal of Semitic Languages*. He tutored. Nan also tried writing, but due to some flaw in the organization of her materials never got far with it. They sold what furniture they could and began to part with his beloved books, an armful at a time.

In the midst of such insecurity, Nan fell in love with a little girl at an orphanage where she went to tell stories, and brought the child home. Anna slept on a cot in the tiny dining room, and called her new protectors Mr. Richardson and (good gracious) Fairy-Godmother.

A practical person would have seen that the situation was unsettled and the effort dubious, but when Aunt Nan's imagination and reality clashed, something had to give, and it was not imagination. Her husband on principle did not believe in saying Thou Shalt Not to another human being. In practice, since he could not give Nan the spiritual and material security which she liked, he could at least allow her to do as she pleased. With his unequaled powers of detachment, he detached himself from the problem.

The difference between a child in the lap on a Saturday afternoon and a child underfoot in cramped quarters soon became clear.

"Never, never again," Nan wrote her mother, "will I undertake such a job, and I thank heaven I have none of my own. Why you did not drown all four of us I don't see, except that we were not half the trouble Anna has been, and were perfectly trustworthy in every way, and never dared to carry on as she has dared to do (this from Nannie of the "usual tantrums") —*and you had more room.*"

After five stormy years Aunt Lillie, the gentle and just, took Anna into her home in Lewisburg, while Grandfather paid her tuition at a girls' school there. A child was not a toy, the Davises said. Once a responsibility had been taken on, someone in the family must meet it. Anna, a practical and sensible girl at heart, trained as a nurse, made a stable marriage, raised a daughter of her own. But Fairy-Godmother had to give up.

Throughout the troubles in Baltimore, many criticized Uncle Dick for bringing them upon himself, but Nan was not among them. In small matters she could be wholly captious, but in this crisis of the soul the ideals which she preached upheld her. She was proud of his courage, she applauded his honesty, she accepted his opinions. During their forty-five years together she reproached him for many things, from sleeping late to talking little, but never in the hardest days or later did she say, "Why did you do it?"

In the end Hilary made a connection with the Unitarians and took a church in Yonkers.

Nan behaved as if removed to the ends of the earth. She dared not make the overnight trip home without a companion, and then only if surrounded by every aid and talisman she could muster: a locket which gave her courage around her neck, her name and address pinned inside her corset, a vial of smelling salts, a small medicine bottle filled with whisky (to be taken by teaspoon), and her Susie Damn doll. This was a two-inch celluloid figure with a weighted bottom which righted itself every time it was knocked over, a potent charm representing the indestructibility of man under the blows of fate, and also a handy scapegoat to slap around in fits of temper.

If no friend or relation could be found to make the trip with her, Uncle Dick had to accompany her himself, his shaggy head lolling from side to side in an agony of boredom, his brow contorted by a migraine headache. The pious pilgrimage home was the only trip she would make, and since she could not live without Dick anywhere else, he was not to travel either. She liked to think of him in a safe place while she was away, surrounded by his books, and never venturing out without his address in his wallet in case of accident.

In Yonkers the Richardsons installed themselves in a railroad apartment at the top of five flights of stairs, from which Nan could never be persuaded to move again. When calls came to larger congregations, they could not be considered.

The flat suited them. Each had a tiny study and a tiny bedroom, in addition to a parlor for formal callers in the front, and a dining room and porch for friends at the rear. The dining table was soon too full of books and papers to serve its original purpose, and they ate, when they ate, on a little table in the kitchen. Meat they avoided, because Nan had a distaste for preparing it. Milk and fruit replaced honey and wild locusts in their fare. They did not fatten.

The books gradually pre-empted not only the dining-room table but the whole apartment. They covered one side of the hall, which was already too narrow; they rose to the ceilings. When Uncle Dick was left alone they took over the front sitting room, stacked waist high on the floor and the chairs. The room had to be abandoned to them.

Living in this congenial confusion, Hilary Richardson used all the time he could spare from his church to embark on a comparative history of religious thought. It was a lifework, unfinished at his death. Perhaps it could never have been finished. It absorbed him into a timeless enjoyment.

Nancy (Nannie or Nan no longer) took over the Sunday

School and the young people's groups with her usual success, and soon had them climbing her stairs at all hours. "I had six for cocoa in the afternoon and five for supper. My pulse was more regular than it has been since I started taking it for Dr. B. I love company." Her liveliness soon also made her many friends outside the church.

Nor was Clarksburg neglected. During her summers there she organized two sets of Campfire Girls, to be carried on by other leaders in her absence, and taught them to call her Poseyemo after a Hiawatha-type Indian messiah whom she dug out of legend. He had left his people with a promise to return. For some reason, perhaps because she was my intimately observed aunt, I was resistant to this particular whimsy.

In Yonkers Nancy put us through her hospital experience. The pronoun refers to her husband, her two sisters, her brother, and myself, to say nothing of a succession of nurses who went past as if on a conveyor belt.

By one of fate's ironies, Nan fell off the platform at Sunday School and broke her hip and her shoulder. Since she had no more tolerance for pain than an infant, the doctors were rapidly reduced to giving her morphine, but she proved to be one whom morphine excites instead of calming. She went out of her mind and so remained for ten eventful days.

There was nothing commonplace in her delirium. Although in traction, she could not be left day or night without a member of her family in the room or she would scream the place down. This was because the nurses were devotees of a strange cult who milked goats at midnight with unholy rites, and who had taken her to a secret temple underground to place her on a stone of sacrifice—perhaps the X-ray table. The light waves reflected on the ceiling convinced her that she was held under water—oh, she was a patient in a million.

Em had a kidney stone attack while this was going on, but

dared not mention such a triviality. Hilary, white as a fish, lunged along like a man carrying a heavy load. Lill, who was fortunately deaf, became more withdrawn daily. The doctor thought the prognosis poor. On my last night of vigil I stood by Aunt Nan's bed all night, explaining away each hallucination as it arose and telling her to come off it. Surprisingly enough, she did, and from then on was merely difficult, but not insane.

In her real and final illness she was tractable and sweet, asked for her mother, dead thirty years, and selected her own epitaph: "Life burned in me with too intense a flame to be extinguished."

That the flame was intense, all who knew her would agree. At seventy-six she was writing, "We are all getting old, doggone it, and I want to be just beginning. It is thrilling to be alive in one of the world's great crises and revolutions. I had a terrible nightmare about the bombs the other night, which always makes Dit perfectly furious. He said no one need yell. As if I had done it on purpose! O!! He has just bought a picture of Erasmus which he seems to enjoy. He says his only family tree is the mental one, and with them around he is never lonely. But what would I do without my human family?"

When her sisters went before her she clung to me as a replacement. It was lucky for all of us that she never had to face the world without "Dit." When he lost her he felt deprived of the fire which had warmed him, yet he endured his solitude philosophically, trying to lose himself in his adventures of the mind.

"I do not think it will be long," he said. "I pray it may not be."

It was both longer and more difficult than he had expected. One night as he walked home from the dinner which he occasionally took in a restaurant, he was struck by a car and permanently lamed. After he came out of his months in hospital, my father sent a young lawyer to take care of a suit for him. Uncle

Dick hobbled down the courtroom aisle to the witness stand and eased himself into the chair with his stick, his bad leg sticking out like a rail.

"Has the injury you received caused you permanent damage, Dr. Richardson?"

"Not at all. Not at all. Leg a little stiff, but getting better all the time. Soon as good as it ever was."

"Was the automobile which struck you proceeding against a red light?" (The police had reported this.)

"I really could not say. It was dark, and I was thinking of something else."

The young lawyer made a last effort to bring his client into line. "Was the car speeding?"

"I would not want to say that. I really did not see him until he hit me. Probably as much my fault as his. Anyhow, I have no hard feelings toward anyone. No hard feelings at all."

The case was dismissed and no damages awarded. The car had not been insured, the driver had a large family—and Uncle Dick had the satisfaction of having hurt no human being by any statement of his.

He was not only unversed in worldly wisdom, he was actively hostile to it. He not only did not make money, he repelled it. He more than suspected that the rich were out to fleece the poor, and he was vociferously on the side of the sheep before the shearer. Both he and Nan bragged to their conservative relations about the protest votes they cast for Norman Thomas. In the Depression, it was of course the Richardsons out of all the family who had their life savings in a bank which failed.

As a pastor, he never allowed his church to hold bazaars, or fairs, or to campaign for money, nor would he make the slightest effort to attract a new parishioner. Congregations came because they liked his sermons, never knowing down which path of man's quest for God he might lead them. He found the church small and he left it little larger, but his people felt that he had given them spiritual food.

When he retired after thirty-five years of service, he received a not excessive pension of seventy-five dollars a month. Only death prevented his giving up the money because of a disagreement with church policy. The Unitarians had become too conservative for him, too hidebound, too illiberal.

His treasures were not laid up on earth, and his wisdom was not of this world. He did not finish his book, but on the day of his fatal fall, he left this page in his typewriter.

Our contention is that the normal human being has within him all the equipment for living the good life that he needs. As Sophocles said in his *Electra:*

"Be strong, my child; be strong.
Out there the Shining One is still great,
Who takes note of all things, and guides,
If we permit it."

In the company of such great minds, long dead, yet truly living, one may train himself into making his science pragmatic;—into an attitude of urbanity, charity, compassion, broadmindedness, toleration; into acceptance as workable fact, though still mysterious, that there is a Power which works in behalf of the good and the beautiful as well as of the true. Thus one may press on toward—the next birthday.

This might well stand as his testament for those who loved him, and in matters of the spirit followed his guidance.

VII

Among all these strongly marked and not incessantly harmonious people, I lived like a mouse under a supper table. I had a frightening amount of attention, yet I found chinks through which I could escape into a life of my own. Since few playmates were approved for me, the house itself became my companion. I was instructed in its use by my two cousins, John and Walter Preston.

At least once a year, with luck twice, Aunt Lillie brought "The Boys" to visit. Since John was nine years older than I and Walter five, they felt a responsibility for bringing me up correctly and they did not neglect it. I saw clearly that it was good of them to put up with me at all, and I was prepared to pay for their company with suffering if necessary.

To gain their approval I would slide down the banisters from the third floor to the first, whizzing around the curves. Naturally this activity had to be carried on without adult supervision, and I was not tempted to try it except when attempting to gain status. Walter also taught me to walk around the house on the gutter.

My dormer windows stared at the courthouse clock over the top of a tall pine tree, and the gutter, a foot wide, ran under them. I had floated paper boats in it after a rain, and that was the only use I had for it, but when Walter climbed out of my window and stood on it, I climbed after him. He started off as if we were on the street, occasionally spreading his arms for balance as though he might soar down into the trees, a Peter Pan in white shirt and knickerbockers, with long black stockings and a round brown head. Between the dormers the roof sloped dizzily and there was nothing to which I could cling. Fortunately, Grandfather had built the gutter as solidly as the rest of the house.

Worse followed. Halfway around Walter climbed to the top of a dormer, then crawled up the slates to the flat square between the chimneys. Was this to be required of me as well?

The crown of the house could be reached from the inside by a ladder and two trap doors, black with bituminous soot like everything else in Clarksburg. My father had taken me there to watch the stars, and even under such safe auspices it was high and fearful. Walter pulled himself over the railing and looked down at me kindly. He was usually kind.

"You had better not try this until you get bigger."

I accepted my reprieve with joy which I tried not to show. He slid down the roof, checked himself on the dormer, landed lightly beside me.

"Now we can go on around."

We did, and to my unspoken horror that was not the end of it. The next time we tried it we were joined by John, who stooped to our company only occasionally. As a big boy he of course had to think of an improvement, which he did by dropping over the edge of the gutter to the roof of the bathroom, thence to the covered back porch, then to the open one, and down a pillar to the ground. Walter was to John as Julia was to Walter, and although I sensed a momentary hesitation in him, he followed. I admired, and longed not to imitate. Again Walter let me off.

"Hang on there until I come back up," he called.

There was no danger of my not hanging on, for I was frozen

to my dormer, but when he reached me I followed him again, bent over my quivering middle. Nemesis awaited us as we crawled through the front window into the hall. Aunt Nan's suspicions had been aroused by voices floating up and down outside her window. She had come up and now discovered that reality was worse than suspicion.

Aunt Nan was excitable, in fact hysterical, although the word was never used. When she was disturbed, and she was easily disturbed, she drowned everyone around her in a spate of words, for like Grandfather, she had the gift of the gab. Grandmother and the rest of the family inclined to the pointed phrase, the succinct sentence.

When she had finished drowning us, she hauled us down to the higher court, which sat in Grandmother's armchair. There it was decreed that we should not play on the top floor for a month. I had the secret disloyal thought that it was better so.

Having lost the roof, we retired to the cellar. In order to make the house stand level on its tilted lot, one side of the cellar had windows, and finished rooms with marble-painted cast-iron mantelpieces. They had been used as dining room, parlor, and kitchen while the house was building. Now they were abandoned and filled with forgotten things.

Walter and I found there properties for our incarnations, wizard and witch, sorcerer and sorceress, genie and ghoul, or on days when imagination flagged, two rather bumbling ghosts. An old buggy tire which the evil witch used for spells became a ring of sanctuary for the benign sorceress.

The black-hearted wizard discovered that the little passage in the cellar could be made completely dark by shutting three doors. We would soften each other up with ghost stories, then each one would take a turn in the passage alone, while the rest howled and scratched outside. If the victim cried for release before the werewolves tired, the wolves had won. The witch felt called upon to survive the test, but a small boy named Willie B. was reduced to tears and scorned.

At dusk, Walter led me up to the top of the orchard behind the house. There, close to the high back fence, the Nameless Terrorer had his lair. His vocation is to chase everyone who runs in the dark.

By daylight the orchard was a friendly place, carpeted with violets in spring and studded in late June by little red and yellow apples of a flavor found only in memory. The trees were suitable for climbing, and under one of them stood my playhouse, with a door so small that no adult could get through it, not even Aunt Nan, who could turn herself into a child like a genie going back into a bottle.

But as darkness crept over the orchard, all the familiar pleasantness vanished. Walter and I would start slowly down the hill, trying not to put ourselves in the Terrorer's power by running. His presence behind us was too much. Soon we were dashing through the long grass, hearing his footsteps thud in unison with our own, feeling his hot breath on our necks. Walter outran me of course. I fell behind, a certain prey, yet somehow reached the kitchen door in time to be saved.

In spite of great efforts, sometimes I acted like a *girl.* One afternoon Walter and another boy decided they were tired of having me tag along and began to pelt me with green apples. I stood the barrage for a while, then fled in unmanly tears, weeping not so much from pain as from rejection, and also from the infuriating inability to throw back straight and hard.

No matter how I tried, at times The Boys had to tell me that I would not do to take along. That is why I was not in the cellar on the day when they made the gunpowder and Walter's friend almost lost his hand.

The Nameless Terrorer was not the only unearthly creature

who haunted our premises. A giant friendly to Aunt Nan lived in the hump which the back stairs sliced out of her room. By rubbing the hump and muttering the proper incantations, she could get him to tell her stories which she repeated to me. I used to be afraid to pass his lair on the way to the bathroom, but actually he never hurt anyone. Like the international situation, he merely threatened. To me, the most obnoxious sprite was the Moon Fairy, who swooped down after people went to bed, gathered the toys they had left out of place, and carried them off to the dark side of the moon. Sometimes she returned them, sometimes not. One day, carrying on my secret life on a level below adult observation, I was disillusioned to find her cache in the sloping recess under the stairs. My hobby horse was there. I cannot imagine how he had galloped so far from his corral in my window alcove as to be in the Moon Fairy's path.

In the midst of these weird denizens the adults lived unperturbed, and so for the most part did I. The Moon Fairy had her hiding place, and I had mine, behind the bookcase in the library window. There I read *The Klansmen*, there I smoked one of Grandfather's cigars, to the lasting detriment of my taste for tobacco, and there I hid from the visiting Presbyterian ministers, many of them bearded, with their deplorable habit of taking me on their knees and asking if I would like to be their little girl. I would NOT.

The cousins never stayed long enough. Aunt Emma and Aunt Nan sometimes turned themselves back into adults, and since I never knew when it might happen, I could not fully count on them. When the silence of the house closed around me, I turned to the dogs and the trees for company.

Into the house Grandfather had put his sense of duty toward his family, sometimes overanxious and oppressive. The trees and the dogs were his joy. He loved to plant, not in a garden as Grandmother did, but on the grand scale—do it once and you do not have to do it again—noble trees and shrubs. He set out the calycanthus bushes on either side of the front porch, and by the time they were twelve feet high we had all learned to imitate his habit of pulling off a wine-red button to crush and smell. The fragrance of that insignificant-looking blossom is still a nostalgic memory. He planted the magnolia, the Japanese honeysuckle, the arbor-vitae, the rhododendron, the bridal wreath, and the mock-orange under the back parlor window where the redbirds nested every year and let us study their family life. Above all he planted trees, and lived to see them grow as tall as his tall house.

I named them for King Arthur's Round Table: the white birch Guinevere, the ginkgo Launcelot, the horse chestnut Galahad. Merlin, large and venerable, stood in the corner by the poplar. The lesser knights, maples, lined the fence, and the King himself, the greatest maple of all, stood alone in the center of the lawn. The elm in the barnyard towered too remote for intimacy. The pines at the gate had no names; they were too different and too gloomy.

The branches of the maple knights started too high for my climbing. Only when The Boys were there could I be hoisted into Guinevere, but in Galahad I could spend hours reading, hidden from the world by the broad fans of the leaves. When I fell because my eyes were on the book instead of the branches, the perfect knight was not to blame.

I made rooms between the roots of the trees, furnished with bark, carpeted with moss, and embellished with wildflowers and bits of colored glass. From my perch on the third floor I heard the trees sing in a variety of voices: the maples brushing softly against the wind, the pine as sibilant as the sea, the horse chestnut a heavy gentle surge, except in winter, when its frozen limbs rattled like swords. Yet there was a monotony in the song of the trees. They spoke, but they could not answer. The dogs knew how to make a response.

My own beloved water spaniel presented me with puppies twice a year, despite all precautions. My elders found this habit deplorable, but I did not. The puppies were far dearer than my motionless and neglected dolls, who were lucky to get out of their beds once every six months. I sat with the puppies when their mother was out and thought that I taught them to eat—an instruction hardly necessary. I caught mange from one litter and my hair fell out in patches, but my love did not falter.

Grandfather could never refuse anyone who came to his office to sell him either a book or a dog, provided the dog were large enough. He accumulated noble breeds such as great Danes, Saint Bernards, Newfoundlands, mastiffs. At one time, due to an influx of puppies, there were thirteen of these lovable monsters on the place. When I tried to ride them, they defeated me by sitting down, and the game ended by my getting licked with a big pink tongue.

But to the delivery boys the dogs had a different aspect. When rushed at by two or three barking animals, each as big as a pony, a boy has a struggle to retain his faith in their essential good will. The telephone would ring and someone would hurry either upstairs or downstairs to reach it, for it hung on the wall in the upper back hall. When Grandfather submitted to the installation of this newfangled contrivance, he took care to place it in the most inaccessible part of the house, where it could not impinge on his life.

"Mrs. Davis, I have your groceries (or ice, or coal); are the dogs locked up?"

"They will be in the back yard, and you may come in the front door."

Grandfather surpassed himself when he acquired June, an

outsize brindle Dane, from a theatrical company which went broke on tour in Clarksburg.

"Not another dog, John!" Grandmother exclaimed, with as much of a groan as her stoicism permitted.

Grandfather looked abashed, but secretly pleased. "She is a fine animal, and they did not have enough money to feed her." This clinched it, since she ate four pounds of meat a day, out of the kettle of scraps that boiled constantly on the back of the stove.

Her role had been to dash across the stage after the comic and tear the seat, well padded, out of his trousers. She was a serious artist who rehearsed every time anyone ran away from her. I discovered that if the quarry turned and spoke to her, she would stop with a puzzled expression, as if saying "wrong cue again." The delivery boys could not take the time to try the experiment. There was a theory that the theatrical manager would return for June, but of course he never did. She had found her home.

The delivery boys are safe now. The big dogs threaten them no longer. It would be lovely and pleasant to go home again, to press the earth so shaded by the trees that it was more cloaked in moss than in grass, to wander through the shadowy rooms, touching familiar things, listening for the voices which were always prompt to answer.

The journey can be made only in memory. The child who lived there has vanished, the great trees are fallen, and all the tongues are still that spoke there. The house itself, built to withstand time, has yielded to the rapacious hands of men. In the name of progress it has been razed and with its surroundings made into a parking lot.

With all of Grandfather's pessimism, his foreboding, his dire predictions as to the future of the nation and of the human race, he could not have foreseen or imagined anything like that.

PART TWO

VIII

All winter I longed for the summer at Media with an eagerness not wholly pleasing to the Davises; but if they felt a jealousy they were far too noble to say so.

Once in my teens when I was complaining about Clarksburg, Grandmother, who had given up the civilized pleasures of Baltimore and never mentioned them, looked at me keenly over her spectacles.

"You and your grandfather had better move. You do not seem to like it here."

Certainly I was not unhappy with the Davises, where I received so much love and learned to love deeply in return. Certainly I do not quarrel with having been taught to use my mind. But I was solitary in that silent house. I dreamed so much there that for years returning was to fall back into dream.

In everyone there is a mingling of both parents, and for the child whose home has not been broken or bereaved, a balanced guidance feeds both sides. I had lost my warm and laughing mother. Without her warm and laughing family a part of me would not have known how to breathe.

For the child I was, Media meant joy and freedom, freedom from anxious supervision, from precocity, from loneliness, from all that in one way or another oppressed my spirit. Children were a commonplace on that farm. No one hung over me, no one seemed to care what I did. I expanded, running wild.

On my first visit Grandmother Davis brought me herself; no one else could be trusted. On my second, Aunt Emma took care of me. By the time I was five, my father arrived with me and left me wholly in McDonald hands.

Young as I was, I felt something lighter in his spirit on that soil, as if with the McDonalds memory became less intolerable. Tears there were plentiful, easily shed, and followed by the warmth of laughter which exorcised their bitterness. Grief there was a living force which watered growth like rain, but did not freeze the roots. John Davis laughed with the clan, was helped by the love and faith which animated them, and held them to him always in a fraternal tie. "A spiritual bath," he called his visits there.

When he came during my stay I would run down the lane to meet him, and he would jump from the buggy to walk up the rise with his arm around me. "Hello there, Betty Brown," he said, referring to my sunburn. I understood that it pleased him to see me running the fields instead of sitting with my nose in a book. He claimed that he had not known a woman who could read Greek and keep her placket closed. He must have exempted his mother from this stricture, for she was always neat in dress.

As soon as the conductor was willing to take me in charge, I made the trip alone, itself an adventure, involving sitting up late, riding overnight on the train, rolling off at dawn at Shenandoah Junction. Uncle Will, who had to get up anyway for the benefit of the tyrannical cows, met me with a big hug. We drove down the dirt road between banks of honeysuckle, dew on the cornflowers, the Queen Anne's lace, the daisies. The birds twittered and flitted through the glassy morning air, and the cattle and sheep, still too drowsy to graze, stared at us from the fields. Little black Maude stepped out in her lively way until the buckboard bounced behind her, and before long we could see the oak woods of Media, dark on the rolling landscape.

I had to open two gates. This was always the prerogative of the youngest passenger, and a relief when my cousin Betty grew old enough to inherit the duty. I carried them back on their sagging hinges, and climbed into the high vehicle as quickly as possible because Maude was fidgeting for her oats. The lane wound for a quarter of a mile through the grove of noble oaks, and the old yellow house stood on a rise at the end of it. In the pasture beyond the trees, where the limestone bones of the land showed through the bluegrass, there were new lambs with new names to be learned. My heart sang all the way. I was at Media again.

Grandfather McDonald stamped out between the bridal bushes to greet me. On the porch Grandmother McDonald folded me in her gentle arms. In the dining room there would be kisses from Mary, Lill, Marshall, John, and probably three or four young cousins, or even children of friends who had been sent to spend a summer in the country with the Major. Aunt Anne herself might break her habit of rising late to welcome me.

It was a home of youth, of merriment, of warm vitality. I can remember great storms in the Valley, sharp cold and baking heat, drought and torrential rains, but my memory has recorded no dull gray days. Clouds could not prevail against so much love and gaiety inside the house.

To be wakened early by the doves in the high oaks, to watch the leaves tossing in shining patterns on the sky, to jump up and look across the fields to the distant wall of the Blue Ridge, is to have drunk in childhood from a well of pure delight.

The mountains were our barometer, sometimes so clear that the separate trees on them were visible, sometimes a blue cloud-bank, sometimes vanishing entirely. They were our guardians, our rampart. Beyond them might lie confusion and danger, but cradled between the Blue Ridge and the Alleghenies the Valley smiled in peace. Or so to a child it seemed.

The Major considered that life was a battle to be fought every day. In Ashby's and Jeb Stuart's cavalry, up and down the Valley with Stonewall Jackson, he had learned something about fighting. Bringing up six boys and four girls, to say nothing of nieces and nephews, kept him from losing his power to command. He ran his family and farm as he had run his troopers. You got your orders. You carried them out without yes, no, or maybe. For failures, for derelictions from duty, excuses were neither expected nor tolerated. The Major had a notoriously low boiling point.

A man of furious energy, he stamped around the place all day on legs slightly bowed from four years in the saddle, his broad straw hat so well down over his eyes that the short white beard was all we saw of him. At eighty he oversaw everything, tended his vegetable garden himself, roared his orders in a voice forever hoarse from the bullet which had lodged in his windpipe. Some people pretended they could not understand him, but they soon found that he could make himself plain. When displeased, he could be heard afar, but his storms were like the thundershowers, violent, soon over, and leaving a freshness in the air.

There were only two people whom his lightning never struck, his loved and loving wife, and myself. My mother's death had left him incapable of disciplining me. She had been his darling, his Birdie of sweet song. I was "little Birdie." When I transgressed he would take me by the hand and lead me to the nearest aunt or uncle, saying, "You scold her. I can't." Fortunately the rest of the family found this so out of character as to be amusing rather than irritating.

On a certain afternoon his battle was with the steam engine which pumped water to the barn, and, second in importance, to the house. This contraption, when it condescended to run, devoured corncobs, turned red with rage, threatened imminent explosion. Bill Perry, a cousin and contemporary, hung around with me to watch the performance, when Grandfather appeared in the door with a bucket and shouted for water.

We willingly took the bucket, but a difference of opinion developed. Bill thought that water was wanted from the horse trough beside the door. I opted for cleaner water from the hydrant near the barn. I won, and we were lurching back with the bucket between us, when Grandfather burst out of the shed like a hurricane. We had been too slow, and his pressure had risen with the engine's.

He seized Bill by the neck and ducked him. "I'll teach you to know a horse trough when you see one!"

I should like to remember that I stepped forward and took the blame. "Grandfather," said the virtuous child, her hand on her heart, "it was my fault." Nothing of the sort happened. Shamefully and ignobly, I fled to the house.

At lunchtime the Major and Bill came in, apparently on good terms. While they washed up and put on their coats, a formality which the boys were not allowed to omit even in the hottest weather, I eyed them warily. Toward the one I had a feeling of guilt, and toward the other of dread, as of thunderbolts.

Grandfather saw me skirting his chair, called me to him and put an arm around me.

"I scared you, didn't I?"

I nodded.

He chuckled. "Water don't hurt little boys."

The Major was a man perfectly balanced by his wife, for to her patience there was no limit, to her angelic gentleness no end. When he stormed, she soothed. It was wonderful to see him roar in, his beard a-bristle, and subside into calm after two words with her. When she faltered, he sustained. Unvaryingly he was there for her to lean upon. She lived for her family, and we let her.

This couple cannot be fully understood without reference to that holocaust of the 1860's which some people call the Civil War. I made the mistake of using this title when talking with my Great-aunt Sue on one of her deathbeds. She sat straight up.

"Never let me hear you call it that, my dear. It was a most *uncivil* war."

"What shall I call it then?" In her condition the word Rebellion would have been dangerous.

"It was the War Between the States," she told me firmly, and sank back on her pillows.

To avoid circumlocution, I shall call it what I heard it called; THE War. Whatever its name, it yawned like a chasm between the youth of my grandparents and the life they built for themselves.

Southerners, and particularly those from that section known for years as United States Military District #1, should have an insight into the minds of occupied peoples anywhere. The inhabitants of the Shenandoah Valley have also known what it means to be invaded, to be occupied, to be taken and retaken, to be defeated, to be ruined, to be oppressed—and to rise again.

By the time I knew the Major and his wife, THE War was merely a flash in an old man's eye, "Dixie" played with spirit on a paper comb to amuse the children, an occasional comrade sipping a julep on the front porch. One of them, wearing a black patch over his eye and still walking like a fighting cock, was named Mosby.

It was much later, piecing together the life stories of my grandparents, that I understood what they had experienced, and what they had surmounted.

Grandfather had of course been deeply affected by his four years of warfare, but his body bore the scars, and not his spirit. He had no incapacity to readjust to the demands of civilian life, even when they were as exacting as many gently reared southerners found them. His change from modest affluence to genuine poverty roused in him a fighting spirit but no complaints. When one way of life closed, he flung himself wholeheartedly into whatever opened. It had been an heroic undertaking to attempt the practice of law, for the bullet at Appomattox had ended forever the hope of courtroom work and confined him to the dustier branches of his profession. When his health broke down under the strain, he put his fighting heart into farming.

He did not bring us up on battle stories. I have learned his from his diary and from the memoirs his comrades wrote. The present engrossed him, demanded all his strength, the past was best forgotten. Occasionally we could coax him into giving the rebel yell, and then even we small ones could see a gleam of something so unlike his ordinary self as to be pleasantly frightening.

It is of course not possible to consign to oblivion a cause for which one has proved oneself ready to die, for which one has sacrificed everything except life. He remembered the Confederacy with passion and tenderness, but he saw it in the light of history. Although I was only eleven when he died, I remember vividly what may have been the only thing he ever said to me on the subject, a comment which set the course of my thinking.

It would have been well for the country if all southerners had reached the same conclusion.

"If I had it to do over again, I should have to fight on the same side, for I could never fight against my own people. But I am glad we did not win."

The most unreconstructed rebel would have to admit that the Major had earned the right to his opinion. He cannot be shown entire unless that aspect of his life is told. When a man has been a part of history, then history must be related.

At the outbreak of war, Edward Allen Hitchcock McDonald was living with his father, stepmother, and seventeen brothers and sisters (yes, seventeen) in a handsome old house on the outskirts of Winchester, Virginia. Winchester had been in the family bones for more than a hundred years since the first McDonald, Angus, came over in 1746 after Culloden, and joined the founders of the town with a grant from Lord Fairfax.

Fighting was in the McDonald bones also, from the highlands of Glengarry down through the centuries, and Edward's father, another Angus, was no exception. He had graduated from West Point, and named his second son for one of his comrades there, who later became a general in the Union army. He had traded furs on the Missouri, fought Indians, re-established himself in Virginia, sired a handsome family, and at sixty considered himself well equipped to lead cavalry in the field. He organized, and for a time commanded, that far from modest outfit called the Laurel Brigade, later led by Turner Ashby.

The first months of the war were a time of excitement and enthusiasm in the McDonald home, young men sleeping on pallets on the parlor floor, fired with the dream of easy victory so universal at the outset of any conflict. The war could not last long, the young men said, because Yankees did not like to fight. Looking back, my great-grandmother quoted bitterly, "Whom the gods destroy they first make mad."

Old Colonel Angus saw nothing as impossible, but the first winter campaign, bivouacking on snow-covered ground, altered this view. Rheumatism took over, Ashby stepped into his place as leader, and into fame.

Young Edward, later the Major, had misgivings about the war from the beginning. To his father's irritation, he had opposed secession. When Virginia left the Union, however, it was not conceivable that he could leave Virginia.

As martially inclined as the rest of his family, he had been colonel of a regiment of volunteer militia. On his way home to call it together, he saw a soldier saying good-by to a pregnant wife, and the woman weeping. A pull at his heartstrings was the only pull that Edward could never resist, for his heart was as warm as his temper was hot. He instantly offered to take the man's place, his offer was accepted, and so he began his service in the Confederate army as an infantry private.

It soon developed that his new captain knew nothing of campaigning. When the company was ordered to take a bridge, the captain turned to McDonald for advice. Mounted on the captain's horse and carrying his sword, McDonald commanded the company with the rank of private, until asked by the authorities to get on with the business of assembling his militia regiment.

By the time he began this, battle lines had been drawn at Manassas. Finding that all of the regiment had enlisted except those of Union sympathy, Edward galloped over to Bull Run himself and joined the cavalry, although just too late for the battle. It was an informal war in those days.

After the battle he again tried to collect his regiment, but could find only forty who were not what he called "unreliable." He got permission to make them into a troop of cavalry and at last joined the Laurel Brigade, where he belonged and where he remained.

These were the young men who circumgyrated the Union army, the eyes and ears first of Jackson and then of Lee. "Their horses jump fences as if they were deer," one irritated northern boy wrote to his family. They had two legendary leaders, Ashby and Stuart. They had a song: "If you want to have a good time, jine the cavalry."

Three times Edward McDonald, a major now, went up and down the Valley with Stonewall Jackson on the campaigns which have become military classics. "Where is the Seventh Virginia?" the Colonel shouted on one occasion. "Here she is, sir," a stout voice answered, but no one could be seen except Major McDonald, hacking his way out of a group of Yankees with his saber.

Following Turner Ashby, the first to take a position, the last to leave it, the Laurel Brigade began to feel themselves unbeatable. Then Ashby took his last of the impossible chances, and lost to death.

The hardened troopers were not ashamed to weep around their campfires that night; but they foresaw no defeat, for they still had Old Jack. "Jackson was transfigured in battle," the Major told my father. "He was the very God of War!" But Jackson fell, shot in error by his own men.

The brigade fought on with J. E. B. Stuart, the last of the paladins, the synonym of courage, of gallantry, with his plumes and his guitar, his singing, and his secret hideaway across the Opequon, a few miles from Media.

By the time the Major reached Gettysburg, he had fought hundreds of skirmishes, been captured, escaped, flouted overwhelming odds. War was a reality now, not a jingle of spurs, the flounce of a lady's dress caught on an unused carbine. Winchester, which was to change hands sixty-two times during the war, had already belonged to the Federal army during two winters.

The McDonald home stood in a sea of mud, the gardens trampled, the trees cut down for firewood, the livestock eaten, the horses commandeered, the servants run off with the Yankees. Edward's stepmother, fighting for the seven small children still with her at home, had saved the house from becoming a smallpox hospital by a direct appeal to a Union general. He then used it as his headquarters, but kindly permitted the family to live on in the attic and to use the kitchen stove along with the soldiers. Mrs. McDonald had seen her youngest baby die of malnutrition. She had saved the others by hiding a cow in the cellar. She had taught her conscience not to scold her boys when they stole a barrel of crackers from a quartermaster's tent, for surely it was better to steal than to starve.

On the long retreat from Gettysburg, Edward McDonald, always thinking of his family, detoured ahead of his command. He galloped up the drive and without taking time to dismount, called his stepmother out.

"If you don't want to spend another winter with the Yankees, you had better leave."

She would go, she could not live through it again, haunted always by the fear that the older boys would lose their tempers and get into trouble. There had been terrible reprisals, and not far away. She managed to borrow a wagon and an old plug. She loaded in six children and everything she could hastily gather. Letting the oldest boy ride the horse, she drove south to Lexington, a hundred miles up the Valley. She never again saw her home, or anything she had left behind.

After Gettysburg the Major rode on for two years, the years of attrition. He slept in his saddle while the tired horse plodded through rainy nights, often he rode thirty-six hours without stopping. His was a branch of the Confederate Army which thought well of itself. Covering country they had known since childhood, they confused the enemy again and again, no march impossible, no odds too great.

But the odds *were* too great.

Ashby was dead, Stonewall was dead, Stuart was dead. In some companies only four of the original comrades remained. And there were more Yankees than ever.

The Major went without food and tightened his belt. His boots wore out and he took a pair from a dead Yankee. His starving horse collapsed on the road. He found another and rode on until a sodden April day at Appomattox Courthouse.

There, in the battle which preceded the unthinkable, the inevitable, a Minie ball ploughed through part of his jaw and lodged against his windpipe. He stuck his thumb in the hole to stop the bleeding and made his way to the house of a friend. The bloodstained scarecrow who could neither speak nor swallow was not recognized at the front door, and sent to the rear. At the back door he made them understand. They put him to bed and sent for a doctor, who came without medical supplies, for there were no supplies left on that side of the line.

"It is a pity," the Major heard the doctor say, "that we must let him die. The operation is too delicate for me to attempt without an anesthetic, and we have none."

The Major made signs for pencil and paper, and wrote his message. "Cut it out. I can stand it."

Now the war was over for the Major, for his short-lived nation, for his heart's home, which was Virginia. It was over for the cause, in which at the beginning he had not believed. He had never owned a slave, and his father had owned only a few house servants. He had opposed secession. He had loved Virginia and fought for her because he could not fight against her.

The war was over, the home gone, the family scattered. Old Angus had died as a result of his treatment in a northern prison.

Edward McDonald had an immediate and pressing need to earn a living; and a total capital of one bony horse. With other equally prosperous cavalry officers, he started a livery stable.

The white men of the Valley were disenfranchised because they had been Rebels. Many at the North said they were lucky not to have been hung. Negroes who could neither read nor write sat in the House of Delegates at Richmond. Only carpetbaggers had money. The Major and his friends were hired to drive a group of Negroes to a social in a country church. It was a wintry night, the festivities prolonged themselves, the drivers came in to get warm.

"Would you gen'lmen mind stepping outside?" they were asked. "You smells so of the horses."

I never heard the Major tell this story. I heard him make only one comment on this period in his life, and that with laughter.

"We had to start from the bottom of the barrel, and the bottom was out."

After a time he managed, with his brother, to rent a house and start a school, bringing two of his sisters to keep house for them. Such little schools were springing up all over the Valley, for the boys had gone into the army before they finished even their secondary education, and all organized schooling was disrupted. While Edward was at Cool Spring, thirty-five, permanently scarred, and penniless, he met Miss Julia Leavell, then nineteen.

She remembered almost nothing except the war and the world which the war had left. It began for her with John Brown's raid, for she was living then, a little girl, near Harpers Ferry. Her mother had died, and her father, a clergyman with a parish in Rappahannock, had taken his five children to his father-in-law's plantation (the local word was "place") where aunts and cousins could care for them.

Some weeks later Mr. Leavell was collecting his mail in Rappahannock when an excited neighbor told him of a slave rising in Jefferson County. A man named John Brown had seized the United States armory in Harpers Ferry only five miles from the Yates place where the children were staying. The slaves had been armed. Colonel Lewis Washington had been dragged out of bed in the middle of the night and carried off as a hostage. No one knew what had become of him. Somebody had been killed. The marines had been sent for.

Mr. Leavell was badly frightened, and with reason. Grandfather Yates was the largest landowner in the county, his place a target if there really were a slave rebellion. The anxious father rode thirty miles without stopping to see if his children were safe.

By the time he arrived, Colonel Robert E. Lee had captured the armory. Colonel Washington, drawing on his green kid gloves, had stepped out free into the sunshine. John Brown's sons were dead. Dead also was the mayor of Harpers Ferry, and a free Negro called Shepherd Hayward, who, ironically, was the first man the raiders shot. There were bodies in the Potomac, and John Brown was in the Charles Town jail.

The slaves had not risen. It was true that they had been armed. I have seen some of the pikes preserved in the old houses. Throughout that savage war, the landowners on isolated plantations, where law rested on conscience alone, suffered no violence at Negro hands. The slaves ran away when they could, but they committed no outrages. It is a tribute to human decency, a decency inherent in both sides, in spite of evil.

After John Brown's hanging at Charles Town, accomplished by due process of law, but a foregone conclusion, the indefensible system of slavery was doomed. There remained only its long death agony.

Julia Leavell was too young to be deeply stirred by these events, or by the outbreak of war two years later. While the nation was welded in tragedy and blood, she spent a girlhood soon impoverished, but gentle and gay.

"Aren't boys fun?" she wrote a friend. "And don't they like to flirt?"

She told me of her first proposal, offered when she was sixteen.

"I was so surprised and excited that I said yes. *Fortunately*, we were on horseback, so we had no time for any embraces. When we got home I ran upstairs as fast as I could to change my clothes. Then I came down and told him I never, never, never wanted to see him again."

It was a blessing for all of us that she did not react in the same way to the Major.

Of material possessions he had precisely none to give her, but neither did any of the other young men whom she would have considered eligible. Their entertainment was to walk together, since walking is free. On one walk he picked up a white quartz pebble, had it polished and set in a thin gold band as a brooch. That was as much as he could do toward an engagement ring.

In 1869 Mr. Leavell retired from the ministry and built an addition to Media, his wife's share of the Yates plantation. The house there had been used for the overseer. Too humble for burning, it had come through the war with no scar except for a hole cut in the floor under a bed so that the silver could be hidden. Three weeks after the Leavells moved in, Julia was married to Edward McDonald in the new parlor.

They started their life together on nothing but love. They ended it, nearly fifty years later, in much the same situation, augmented by a family of ten children and a big mortgage on the farm. During those years they found a happiness so glowing that others felt it instantly, and also an immoderate amount of grueling hard work.

"I came to bread-making with tears," my grandmother told me once—and laughed.

The Major took his bride to Louisville, where he hoped to practice the law that he had somehow found time to read. "I walked out on an unfinished bridge over the Ohio," she wrote. "The wind almost blew me off, but I am a real western woman now, and not afraid of anything." The babies kept coming, Edward, Anne, Julia, Will, Angus, Percy, Mary, Marshall, John, Francis.

"God has been very good to me. For twenty years I was never without a baby in my arms."

There is a photograph of the young mother holding her firstborn, her lovely face full of sweetness and dignity, her dark hair, so long that she could sit on it, coiled in a crown on her head. After that the children were photographed alone. Mama had neither time nor taste for posing.

All of them were born in Louisville except Marshall, who arrived one summer when they were at the farm. Perhaps that is why he loved it more than all the others did. When little Francis died of "summer complaint," his place was filled by Lill, the orphaned daughter of a brother.

Mrs. McDonald had enough to do. A letter describes getting the clan ready for an Easter Sunday. Ed boasted a new suit. Will had Ed's old one, Angus had Will's, Percy had Angus's. Marshall wore trousers of Percy's which had been cut down. John, in kilts, and Francis, in the cradle, were left at home. Anne had a new hat, Julia wore Anne's old one. Mary had new hair ribbons. "As for myself, I indulged in a new pair of gloves, which I did not have time to put on until I reached the church door."

The six sons, energetic and fearless, covered a great deal of ground, and are said to have been known in Louisville as "those bad McDonald boys." "Find out what Angus is doing and tell him to stop," became a family byword. The boys discovered that after the workmen left a building which was under construction near their home, they could climb the scaffolding and swing down on a rope from the third story to land on the roof of a horsecar as it trotted past. This required timing, but was good sport until the evening when Angus—or was it Percy, the future clergyman?—saw the face of his father among the startled passengers peering out of the car window. He was hauled in and summary discipline instantly administered.

"You cannot bring a McDonald up without spanking," the Major said, and he was in a position to know.

But he was not all disciplinarian. When he came home in the evening and found the house boiling and his gentle little wife "ready to jump into the Ohio," he would collect the children, provide them with cake tins, spoons, any possible noisemakers, herd them into an empty room, and invite them to see who could make the most racket. After fifteen minutes of bedlam they were usually willing to be quiet.

The exigencies of her life developed Grandmother's natural calm. With the Major to provide the sterner side of authority, her strongest admonition to the children could be "Don't think about yourself."

In this she took her own advice. It is true that in the deepest sense she never needed to think about herself. She never had to question her position in the family, to wonder if her life had meaning, to establish her own importance. On one of the summer hegiras to Media, she got left behind on a station platform talking to a friend. The shrieks of nine children were better than an alarm signal. The conductor made haste to stop the train and back up for her.

Although her life was not easy, it had a solid foundation—the Major's love. For this she gave up independence, and never thought of it as an exchange.

Twenty-one years married, he was writing her: "My precious wife, you can give any of your visitors advice on how to run a household with the smallest percent of friction and the least help. You have many talents and accomplishments, but none more commendable in a mother of nine. I am glad to think I shall spend but one more Sunday without you."

On their twenty-eighth anniversary, according to their daughter Julia, "they held hands, sang love songs, and discussed the wedding as if it had been only last year."

It would be too much to suppose that they never disagreed. At least once she opposed him, and over the oak trees. They had returned to Media, the Major was battling to keep the family fed and to send the boys to college. He brought in a sawmill and began to sell lumber. She protested. He continued. She could not bear it in silence.

"Your Papa is more cheerful and enterprising than ever, after all his losses from cholera, short crops, and incidental expenses, and forges ahead at one thing or another all the time. He has installed a sawmill. I fear he is making inroads on our beautiful forest." Then she added a staunch conclusion, a loyal wifely note. "Anything to pay the notes as they fall due at the bank."

Perfectly aware of her feelings, the Major could not allow himself to be deflected.

"I think your Mama hopes that I am improving the forest. Although she regards each tree as one of her ancestors."

They might differ, but differences could not divide them, for at heart they shared the same ambition.

Wrote the Major: "In my own life I have been greatly blessed in health, home, family, and surroundings. I have not achieved greatness nor acquired wealth, but I would not exchange the first for the last."

Wrote his Julia: "To be loved is worth more than anything

John W. Davis and Julia McDonald when engaged and seven years later, when they were married

Grandmother McDonald with her first of ten; Major McDonald of Jeb Stuart's cavalry

The uncles, always "The Boys," and a few of the clan (BELOW)

Myself, slightly younger

"Media," where the McDonalds lived

The oaks were our home

The Davis house went straight up in the air

A group of unrepentant individualists

Grandfather Davis with a serious thinker

The Embassy Girls at Cannes

Caught leaving our embassy in in Chesham Place, London

The Davises with Lloyd George at Chequers for "The Prime Minister's Housewarming" (ABOVE); *the Davises with Winston Churchill* (BELOW LEFT); *the Ambassadress* (BELOW RIGHT); *and the American Ambassador* (OPPOSITE PAGE)

Champion for a Day—accepting nomination in Clarksburg, 1924 (ABOVE); *three good Democrats—Roosevelt, Davis, Smith* (BELOW LEFT); *and content in the practice of law* (BELOW RIGHT)

else in this world, money or lands or luxuries. We should thank our Heavenly Father for *family* affection."

Their ambition was fulfilled, for family affection they had in full measure, and both were carried to their graves by six strong sons.

"I had rather have that guard of honor," said my father to his solitary daughter, "than a regiment and a military band."

IX

It was fortunate that the Major and his Julia cared more for family life than anything else, because what they ran at Media was a youth hostel. The young people might sleep three in a bed, or overflow to mattresses on the floor. Adult guests had to be close relatives who did not mind doubling up. Twenty-four could be packed into nine bedrooms, but none might be refused. That was the code. Many came, and some were Tartars.

"Run! Run and hide!" the children shouted. "Cousin John is coming up the lane!"

On he came, as fat as Samuel Johnson, his light buggy sagging so perilously under his weight that we vainly hoped he would upset. It did no good to hide, for he always stayed for the next meal, eating a plateful of Grandmother's rolls, which he seized three at a time. He would catch us with his pudgy hand, expect a kiss on his red face, invite us to sit on the alpine slope which had been his lap. Then he would send us to pick sweet peas for the young lady on whom he designed to call that evening, for he still saw himself as a dashing beau.

Girls used to hide under the bed when they saw him coming. He had been known to present his flowers to one charmer at night and thriftily gather them from the parlor table next morning to take to another down the road. He had enough money to live without working, which Grandfather thought a curse.

Grandfather called John's sister Blizzard Net, because she always arrived before a storm which would prevent her departure. She made a career of visiting. Invited once for Thanksgiving dinner, she stayed until Easter. When she died it snowed so hard that her coffin could not be moved out of the church for three days. This surprised no one in the family.

She had delusions of grandeur because her older brother had returned to England to inherit a family estate. By leaping from branch to branch she climbed the family tree to William the Conqueror, wrote all her letters on creamy crested paper, and charged about among her kin, telling them where they failed to live up to their line. When my mother married my father, she was impelled to remark that it was sometimes well for the aristocracy to marry with the yeomanry.

One of her English nephews came over for the summer and every night left his shoes outside his door to be blacked. This so entertained my uncles that they took turns getting up to do it.

These were Grandmother's relatives. Great-aunt Sue was a McDonald and took no bright view of the meek gentility practiced by the other side of the family. When the cousin who had inherited the "big house" left it to be sold for the benefit of educating indigent young men for the ministry, Aunt Sue called it "encouraging mediocrity." She had more than her share of what she called Highland pride, and what irreverent outsiders referred to as "that terrible McDonald temper."

"Sue is coming to stay for a month," Grandmother said. "I hope we all behave like Christians."

A beautiful old lady with a straight back, wavy white hair, a skin like the inside of a shell, in her eighties she used to lie down for an hour before going out to dinner, with a cold cloth over her eyes to make them shine. Having been a beauty, she gave herself the airs of one, and woe to any clod of a nephew who did not spring up to pull out her chair.

Aunt Sue was unreconstructed. When a *Republican* tried to shake hands with her, she folded her hands behind her back.

"It's a pity you have to live in New York," she told me, "among those Vanderbilts and Astors, those new rich who are ruining our country." Informed of my impending marriage to a man named Adams, she tilted her delicate nose and murmured vaguely, "Adams? Adams? They are nice people, aren't they?"

At one time she came to Media to end her days, but it took too long and the rooms were too draughty. Furthermore, both she and Aunt Anne were all McDonald. After a number of spirited clashes, Aunt Sue retired to a room in town which she kept at blood heat, and entertained herself by altering her will as various nieces and nephews incurred the sunshine of her approval, or the blasting fury of her wrath.

There is no introduction to the vagaries of human nature like that of growing up in a large family.

Media in those days was not so much a house as a way of living. Far into my childhood it still had none of the conveniences now considered necessary—plumbing, heating, electricity. We did not know that we were ill-housed and underprivileged. We thought we had "a lovely home."

With the ease of flicking electric switches, something has been lost. There is a mystery, a beauty, in walking from room to room with a lighted lamp, seeing the wavering shadows clot in corners from which they fly at your approach, only to close in behind, unvanquished, threatening still. Then to set the lamp down and create a golden island in the darkness, a circle of safety; to be oneself the source of light.

When the little girls went to bed, a lamp was left for them on the floor in the upstairs hall. We crawled out in our nightgowns and made shadow play with our fingers. Sometimes we laid things across the chimney to watch their pattern on the ceiling. A hole burned in a sweater gave us away.

No one could romanticize the washstand, but at least it never got out of order.

In spite of these drawbacks, company kept coming. My mother had seventy-two first cousins. Cousins arrived or sent their children—*all* their children—for the summer; cousins brought their aged mothers to die at Media. Nephews arrived at night unannounced, crept upstairs, and appeared at breakfast. I never realized until grown and married that entertaining cost anything. The farm fed us, and our food was never charged against it. Of course we ate what was in season. Thus I came to know the ghastly productivity of the string bean. Strawberries taken three times a day will produce hives, but nothing tastes so good as licking the dasher from an icecream freezer in which top cream has been slightly sweetened and flavored with vanilla —unless it might be butter, fresh from a barrel churn.

The visitors helped with the work, but physical work, done with a congenial team, can promote companionship as well as golf or tennis can. Except at the peak of the harvest, an afternoon could be stolen for a picnic at the river, or the parlor cleared and waxed for a dance, with Grandmother or Aunt Anne at the piano. If McDonalds could not be brought up without spanking, neither could they be brought up without fun. Every night, party or not, we sang until the peacock screamed.

All of this merriment rested squarely on the stooped and slender shoulders of Mrs. McDonald. Without losing her gentle smile or raising her soft voice, she kept us fed. Toil gnarled her hands but did not whet her disposition. With wonderful charm of manner, with the most graceful hospitality I have ever seen, she made visitors feel that she expected them to stay for weeks or months, and many of them did.

Two people on the farm rose at five thirty, Grandmother and Uncle Will. The Major, no sluggard, did a number of chores before seven o'clock breakfast, and expected the same of his sons. Mary and Lill were prompt to help, but Anne, the rebel, slept until a lazy eight. No one called the little children. They were driven to the table by hunger and an eagerness to start the adventures of the day.

Before we assembled, Grandmother had cut up a mountain of fried apples, set out the cold ham, the dish of hot boiled eggs, the fresh rolls ready to run with butter, the preserves, the oatmeal, the clabber, the milk, the cocoa, the big silver pot of coffee. All this she produced on a wood range in a kitchen without running water.

We washed the dishes in the long passage, with two dish pans and two boiling kettles, but when we came to the pots and pans she told us, in the language of her wartime girlhood, "You are honorably discharged."

As we scattered to do the housework, or get garden produce ready for exchange at the store, she sat down to peel potatoes as for an army, to shell a thousand peas, to make up more rolls from the dough set to rise the night before.

In the afternoon she rested for an hour, reading her Bible in the sunny window of the dining room. On Sunday she took her weekly outing. In her black silk dress, in her bonnet with the flowers under the brim, she was driven to church in the surrey, with any other members of the family who cared for the privilege. The rest of the time she worked, but her work was animated by a conscious philosophy.

"My life is spent in the trivial round, the common task, but it must be what the Master thinks I am fitted for, and I do it with all my might, putting more time and strength on it than necessary perhaps, but it makes home attractive, and I love to have it so."

Being, as was her only boast, the daughter, sister, and mother of an Episcopal clergyman, she would have liked more church work. She had to let her children do it for her, writing her daughter Julia: "The Bishop spoke warmly of you and Ed as church workers, a great encouragement to such a barren fig tree as your mother, who thinks maybe after all she has not lived in vain—and there is Percy too."

Even with their family to serve, my grandparents might have found their poverty more grueling but for an advantage which today's scattered refugees lack. Their friends and neighbors were in the same condition. They could laugh with old acquaintances about the days when "a lady in the kitchen was like a blooded horse at the plow," and a gentleman never used a hoe.

Some of the acquaintances tried to turn back the clock by living in nostalgia, but not the Major and his wife. In our county, Jefferson County, one said, "They are rich, *but* they are nice people." The combination was rare enough to deserve astonished comment. In addition to that, Jefferson, with its neighbor, Berkeley, had to be more southern than the South. They were, and are, the Alsace-Lorraine of America.

History had touched them heavily, as it touched the McDonalds. Not only had the war marched back and forth across them, but in the midst of this disagreeable process, they had been riven from their mother state, Virginia, by an unnatural means called a plebiscite.

The Federal army was in occupation; the Baltimore and Ohio Railroad did not wish to run in Confederate territory. The Federals rounded up the only seventy voters left in the county, Union sympathizers all, since the other men were fighting for the C.S.A. They voted the counties into the new Union state of West Virginia, which had set up a government in Wheeling, beyond the Alleghenies.

The people of Jefferson laughed, but they laughed too soon. The war ended, and they were still West Virginians. Virginia sued to get the counties back and lost twice in the Supreme Court of the Reconstruction Era. Citizens of Jefferson who tried to vote for Virginia legislators were forcibly restrained by the Federal troops still occupying the county after the surrender.

Not until 1871, after the second Supreme Court defeat, did the local paper, *The Spirit of Jefferson*—still extant—put West in front of Virginia on its masthead. This step was accompanied by an editorial:

> WEST VIRGINIA BY FORCE AND FRAUD
>
> West Virginia can offer no price which would prompt us to submit willingly to the deep damnation of our taking off from our dearly loved mother.

Fifty years later, the people of Jefferson were still proudly unassimilated. "When are you going back to West Virginia?" friends asked me sweetly. During World War I, the Stars and Stripes were at last hung out again on Charles Town houses, but they were crossed with the Stars and Bars.

(It is only fair to say that by World War II the United States flag ruled alone. Little is left of the old agony except a deep distrust of plebiscites.)

Tutored by the Major, the McDonalds did not strike these attitudes. Percy and Marshall went to France in 1917 with no commotion about the Confederate flag. The family changed with their times, and so did the house they lived in.

This old house, which was and is so much loved, has its eccentricities. It was never planned, but improvised according to needs, growing by the work of many hands, some as anonymous as a coral polyp. The Davis house was a monument to one man. The monument has perished, the improvisation survives. No one can adapt a monument.

Before records were kept, an unknown man of enterprise cut down enough trees to build a two-story log cabin and a smokehouse. He chinked the rough-hewn logs with Shenandoah mud, which is chiefly clay, and used a ladder to reach his second story. Whoever he was, he had a fine sense of location. The house sits well, and the oaks around it are survivors of the original forest.

Someone else added a wing of rough limestone drawn from the fields. There is a theory that Hessian prisoners of war did most of the early stone work in the Valley. They may have worked at Media. In any event, when John Yates owned a thousand acres his overseer still had to go upstairs by an outside staircase. The cellar under this part of the house has always flooded, and modern science has not been able to overcome the habit.

Great-grandfather Leavell sliced up enough oaks to make the siding for an American Gothic front. He liked building in the most up-to-date style of his day, but lack of funds saved him jigsaw decoration, except for a modest scallop under the eaves, and one gable window, which lights precisely nothing. At least he did contrive a graceful inside staircase. The oak planks have shrunken and the wind blows through the chinks. Aunt Mary used to fill in around the windows with newspaper forced in by the back of a knife. We use putty now.

The logs, the stones, the planks still form the house. Built by native labor out of native materials, it may truly be said to have grown out of the earth on which it stands, and so have the family which live in it.

In the old days there were so many of us. Anne was the eldest at home. Having no patience with anyone, she required the most patience from others. Even the Major admitted that he could not do anything with Anne. The energy she spent in not conforming to the family pattern might have accomplished great things if she had had a life of her own. She had all the McDonald emotionalism and no wish whatever to bring it under control.

Tall and pretty, with fair curly hair and flirtatious blue eyes, she liked to study, she was ambitious, she won a gold medal for her music at school. (When that happened the Major had a silver one made and gave it to Julia for helpfulness at home.) There could be no education for her after high school; too many brothers pressed on her heels. Then deafness came upon her and cut her off further from the world.

She did not suffer in silence. She did not partake of the daily chores. After breakfasting in queenly solitude, she might bake a cake, or keep a dish full of fudge, but someone else made her bed, and neither she nor anyone else picked up her clothes. With the absolutism of youth, I disapproved of her, but looking back she seems like a strong and beautiful tigress in a cage too small.

"Strenuous" was her favorite word. "Child," she would say, pressing my hand and rolling her eyes heavenward, "farm life is *strenuous*." Her tears were always ready to flow, and her laughter lay directly under them, so that at times even she did not know whether she was laughing or crying. When her movements became unusually quick and jerky, we knew that storm signals were up. Flushing and streaming she would rise and denounce us all, even reproaching Grandmother for having allowed her to be born, and reducing that gentle soul to tears, while Will, her favorite target, looked stolidly at his plate. Then she would rush to the back yard and thrash down weeds with a sickle until she was red and panting, or retire to her room and make the house reverberate with the bang of her closing shutters.

Only Marshall, something of a time bomb himself, knew how to handle her. If he were present, he would lead her away with his arm around her and walk her up and down under the oaks, her head on his shoulder, until she subsided.

No one could resist him, bonny, brave, warmhearted Marshall, with a smile which charmed the world and a dimple made by a scar on his cheek. Like a big brother, he took me to my first dances and made sure that I enjoyed them; illegally and thrillingly he taught me to drive his Model T, the first car on the farm. He served on the chief engineer's staff in France and then returned to Media, for he was rooted there like the oaks. In the end great sorrows came upon him, and his life had a ring of Greek tragedy, a loyal man enchained by loyalty, a generous man undone by generosity, a brave man defeated by his inability to give up. But in my sun-drenched childhood on the farm, those days were far away.

With devilish ingratitude, because she was the one who did most for me, I teased Mary. In every large family there is one who bears the heaviest load. When my mother died, Mary took her place. Since she fought her way up in the midst of brothers, she was known as the little Indian, but she grew into a happy blend of Yates gentleness and McDonald scrappiness. Her beaux were my meat. When she was entertaining one in the parlor I planted myself with a contemporary on the front porch. Two heads, one yellow, one red, rested on the window sill, and not even promises of candy could make them go away.

She married Robert Browse, in spite of the trouble we took to hide her five pictures of him every night and pretend to be asleep while she hunted for them. He became my explosive, intelligent, affectionate Uncle Bob, and took her away from us, but only as far as the next farm, which he bought because she did not wish to leave the Valley.

The Valley is a Circean part of the world which fastens dangerously on the heart. Its children go away, but they return. John traveled widely, earned four degrees, and came back to walk the land and speak Latin to his beeves and apple trees. *Opus fervet,* he says happily. The most unassuming man alive, he may be summed up in a single incident. After he had been married for ten years, he took his wife to a reunion at the University of Virginia.

"Would you like to go to the Phi Beta Kappa dinner?" he asked. "They usually have good speakers."

"But John, you can't go to that unless you are a member."

"I am." It was the first she had heard of it.

With childhood's unerring instinct for the buttered side of the bread, we children tagged after Will. "Will may not get far on earth," Grandmother said, "but he is sure of a front seat in heaven." If the virtues of patience, humility, kindness, obedience, love, are the keys to the door of a single pearl in the wall of chrysoprase, then she was right. He would do anything for us, saddle the horses, show us the new calves, tell us where the cat had littered, let us use him for a jungle gym.

He would take us with him on the reaper, clattering through the golden fields, or on the hay wagon, deep in the fragrant load. Our days were long and lovely, each with its own excitement. No one regimented us. We took on such congenial tasks as carrying out a bucket of lemonade to the men in the hot fields, or feeding the twin lambs from a bottle. Even the thunderstorms were a glory.

As they gathered work stopped, the men came in, we sat it out together in the parlor. The dogs were admitted for the emergency, and the collie went from one to another, saying his prayers by laying his paws on a human knee and dropping his nose between them, begging his helpless gods to end it. The beagle found a properly occupied chair and crawled under it. Great balls of fire was no mere exclamation in those storms. I have seen them roll in one window and out the other. If it got too bad, Grandfather read prayers for us. He often held prayers for the family anyway, and no one was allowed to be self-conscious about getting down on his knees.

When the vortex of the storm moved away, the count of six between the flash and the thunder lengthened to twelve or to eighteen, the rain fell in a curtain which blotted out the barn, and we children rushed into the downpour with our clothes on, barefoot and shouting. A row of hens huddled along the porch clacked disapproval, the peacock had vanished, dragging his stately tail, the guinea fowl had taken to the woods, the squirrels and the birds were in hiding. Nothing stirred except ourselves, wild, storm-possessed, and free.

The McDonalds had such practice in putting up with all sorts of people, that they were able to put up with me, although their stories of my early life are not engaging. When I lay on the floor sucking a bottle and reading a book, when I pushed into the crowd around the piano and announced that I would rather sing by myself, when I selected a volume called *The Mazes and Phases of Love* to squash a bug, they found me funny. With perfectly unfeigned laughter, without coaxing or correction, they brought me into line. Faced by their kindly but united chorus, I learned to behave like other people, to read less, to work more, to be one of a team.

It was in my early teens that I felt most the relaxation of being at Media. "Child," they said on my arrival, "we must get you some beaux."

The dayton would go to town behind the fat-backed, slow-moving horses, and come back loaded with adolescents of both sexes to spend the night. We were about twenty years behind the times. Lack of money and nostalgia for a vanished past had kept the mores stable. Our dances required only a victrola and a bowl of lemonade, and most of the boys who took me to parties were horse drawn.

The ride home could be the best part of the evening, the horse plodding at its own pace through the resting countryside, the soft night noises of the tree frogs, katydids, and crickets, the moon and stars to watch in their clear beauty, undimmed by artificial light. Soothed by the rhythm of the steady hooves, the creak of harness, the scrape of the wheels on the dirt roads, we let conversation lapse, sank timelessly into the night. When we reached home we were not greeted by a reception committee as in Clarksburg, Aunt Emma agitated at the front door, Grandmother questioning on the stairs, Grandfather the heavy artillery in the upper hall. All the dear Medians wished to know next day was, "Child, did you have a happy time?"

It was an easier life to control than that of the present. The boys were cousins, connections, or grandsons of Grandfather's friends, brought up to feel a sense of responsibility which there was no doubt their families would enforce. A girl was supposed to set the tone of a relationship, and her decision was not questioned. The boys who drank on social occasions were exceptions to be avoided, and the girls who drank were simply not behaving like ladies—the ultimate condemnation. I have said that we were twenty years behind the times, but perhaps it was more.

Neither of my grandmothers ever mentioned morals to me; they would have thought the subject indelicate. Long ago and far away as if in another country, they did instruct me in manners.

"A Virginia lady," said my sweet Grandmother McDonald, "always sits with both feet on the floor, her hands folded in her lap, and her back not touching the back of the chair. She never thinks about her appearance after she leaves her bedroom."

"I hope you will make many friends in life," said my positive Grandmother Davis, "but remember that you will never know any of them well enough to enter their houses by the back door, or to poke their fires." It is a good basis for friendship when you think it out.

But as slowly as we moved into the twentieth century, modernity did catch up with us at last. Some conveniences began to appear. "The telephone is an assistant, but it is also a hustler," Grandmother said. When necessity forced her to answer it she would seize the receiver with a forced courage, stand as far away as the cord would reach, and scream toward the mouthpiece.

Running water was introduced—fitfully—into the house, electric light bulbs hung nakedly from cords in the ceiling, Angus installed a hot-air furnace, which he described in disgust as "as warm as a cat's breath."

Most material blessings came from the distant uncles: Ed, who had much of his mother's capacity for never doing wrong, a lawyer in Lexington, Angus, a lawyer in Charleston, Percy, a rector in Montgomery. They made their lives elsewhere, but visited often, were met with rejoicing, and never lost their clan spirit.

(What this could mean I learned later in life, when I had made some serious mistakes. Thoughtfully, although with affection, the Davises inquired into them, as they inquired into everything, to analyse and to discover how such things could be. The McDonalds simply closed ranks around me.)

When Angus came to visit the family turned to him like sunflowers to the sun. He was as comfortable to sit beside as a well-banked fire, and he was so funny! His rendition of *The Burial of Sir John Moore*, or of *The Huckleberry Picnic*, are deathless to anyone who heard them. With it all, he had a most un-McDonald capacity for making money. It was he who later installed Aunt Anne in a house in town, where she was comfortable for the first time in her life and went on weeping sentimental tears about the joys of Media (Mama was so *sweet* and Papa was so *brave!*). Angus paid all the bills that were hard to pay, covered all the emergencies, and left his money to his wife with the understanding that she would turn it into a trust fund for his brothers and sisters, which she did, showing a generosity of spirit equal to his own.

All of the visiting uncles had sweet voices, which added greatly to our evening music. In all the memories of Media, the evenings are the most clear.

When the hot sun sank, and the cool breeze stirred the oaks, we hurried through our cold supper, for the main meal was always in the middle of the day, and went out to enjoy ourselves. Twilight gathers slowly in that latitude, and the dusky air is drenched with honeysuckle. The lawn was a clearing ringed by trees which no man planted, and their tall tops made another clearing in the sky where the stars gathered like fireflies over a dark lake.

So long as we could see, we played games or tried feats of strength. The little boys could skin the cat on Will's iron arm, golden Marshall would carry dark Mary standing on his shoulders. If Angus were there we would call on him for his repertoire, with gestures which he outrageously claimed had been taught him by his elocution teacher.

When the lake of the sky sparkled thickly with stars, we drew chairs into a circle and sang, songs both traditional and comic. Could the voices have been as sweet, the harmonies as true as I remember them? The peacock raucously joined the chorus, while the dark world rustled around us and our eyes focused on the one patch of light, the golden window of the dining room through which we could see Grandmother and Grandfather reading by the oil lamp on the table, and occasionally exchanging a word in the contentment of complete understanding. They gave us their peace.

New saplings now grow in the woods at Media, a new set of stubby little feet now run about under the oaks. The new generation will make their contribution to the family annals. If they look back, they can find almost any sort of behavior behind them. If some among us took strange paths, we repudiated that individual no more than the apple tree repudiates the blemished apple. They were a part of ourselves, neither less nor more.

On an old farm walked by generations of the same blood, it is not possible to die. It is possible to feel only the transmutation, the continuity of life. The flower blooms, becomes a seed, ripens, casts its treasures on the ground. It has not died. It has fulfilled itself, passed on its essence, made it possible for coming flowers to bloom. Some blossoms are fairer than others, but all partake of the absolute, which is Flower itself.

So in an old house, much lived in, there are ghosts. The influence of those who have dwelt there can be felt, even by newcomers who did not know them, as fragrance passes from one year's roses to the next. We accept the absence of our forerunners, for they have made room for us, have made it possible for us to spend our hour in the sun, to reach our fruition under the sky. We accept too the fact that some day each of us will join them, will become a member of the company of those friendly ghosts.

PART THREE

X

With two stable homes, with so much being loved and loving in return, it is not surprising that my father's move to Washington made little immediate difference in my life. He had been so often away, so busy, so abstracted, so full of unspoken sadness, that at first he seemed hardly more absent than usual.

I once announced that I loved God, Daddy, and Uncle Percy, but I loved Uncle Percy the best. This view was subject to radical revision later on, but reflected my infant mind.

In later years I saw my father helpless before the charms of little blond girls such as I had been, and playing with them delightfully. Whenever he tried to play with me, something went wrong. Once he carried me downstairs on his shoulder—it could not have been the only time—and fell. My foot caught and twisted in the balusters. It was Grandmother and Aunt Emma who applied the antiphlogistine, while he fled.

The pony did not perform her expected function of giving us something to do together. On an early ride, when I was just beginning to savor the pride of being off the leading rein, Nellie decided to gallop down a precipitous hill, and the ground flew up and hit me. As I lay there in surprise, I heard my father calling from afar, not "Darling, are you hurt?", but "Catch that horse!" I struggled up and did so before he reached me.

Driving went no better than riding. On our first triumphal progress in the pony cart, Nellie stopped on Fourth Street near the Episcopal church. Admonishment did not move her, a gentle tickle with the whip she ignored, a sharp blow also. When Father tried to lead her, she lay back in the traces. As his temper rose so firmed her decision that putting one foot in front of another could only lead to having more of it to do.

At last he ordered me out of the cart to walk home. While I stood bemused on the sidewalk, he leapt in and laid about her until she ran up one street and down another. Shortly after this episode, in which the town was treated to the spectacle of a wild man in a jaunting cart flogging about the streets a pony scarcely larger than a dog, Nellie found a new home and vanished from the family scene.

I thought it far easier to be taught to ride at Media by Nancy, a half-bred mare of infinite patience. "I told you children not to race those horses," the Major would say, "and then I see you tearing over the fields like Comanches," but he was himself too much a horseman to disapprove seriously. Nancy carried us, sometimes in turns, sometimes three at once, until she had had enough of us, giving full value. Then she went back to the barn and scraped us off at the low door. End of ride.

With the pony or without her, I longed to see more of my father, but then I always had, there was nothing new or startling in that. When I was eleven, however, an event occurred which made a vast and basic change in the whole pattern. He remarried.

He told me of it on the day it was to be. I wept. I could not say why I was weeping, but I wept all day. He assured me that he would not love me less, that "Miss Nellie," whom I knew only as having dressed a doll for me, was eager to give me a mother's love, that we would be more together in the future than in the past. Still I wept.

I sat on his lap and wept, until at last he disentangled himself from the sodden child to go to his office. He was to leave for Washington immediately after the ceremony, and last arrangements had to be made. I sat at the lunch table and wept, played with paper dolls and wept, huddled by the fire and wept. Grandmother and Aunt Emma tried to comfort me. I would not have to leave them, they said. Daddy would still come home on visits from Washington. Nothing would be changed. I knew better. I was right, of course, but it was not an unselfish way to send him off into a new happiness which he well deserved.

This marriage, unlike the other, had been preceded by the stormiest family objections. Although it had been under consideration for more than a year, when it took place Grandmother had only just been brought around, Grandfather was as disapproving as Moses when he broke the Ten Commandments, Aunt Nan had laid the groundwork for a feud which never healed. Only Aunt Emma felt at the last minute that John must have some of his family with him, and made the third witness in the pastor's study.

The new Mrs. Davis was the daughter of John Bassell, a Clarksburg lawyer who was considered Grandfather's opposite number in the profession. She was the eldest of five sisters, as beautiful and lively as the Langhornes, who made their house the gathering place of the gay young people, in so far as Clarksburg had them. Any young man, John Davis included, who dropped in of an evening, could be sure of a welcome from lighthearted company. He had availed himself of this pleasure like the rest.

They drank beer, danced, played cards. Julia McDonald had

done all those things, and when she came to Clarksburg had liked the Bassell girls very well. But Nell had been *divorced*, a shocking thing in that time and place. Her reasons had been so mandatory, her husband such a scoundrel, that the divorce could not be held against her, but remarriage was another matter. When John first told his family of his plans, Grandfather hung his opposition on that. Announcements ready to be sent were packed away in a trunk in the Bassell attic. Then the first husband died, and John and Nell decided to go ahead.

Actually, the Davises were objecting to more than the divorce. They thought the Bassell girls aspired to lead the fast set and would rather be called *swagger* than anything else. They considered Nell worldly, ambitious, extravagant. They might have added that she was proud, quick-tempered, easily offended. She was all of those things, and she made my father a devoted and helpful wife for thirty-four years. At last he had someone to drive him—not to work, for that he never needed, but in other ways.

Their courtship had been so protracted that I must have been the only person surprised by the marriage. In April, a year and a half before, John wrote his mother of "the weight of personal worry and distress which has crushed me for the past year."

"I blame myself for calling up the subject and worrying you, while on the other hand you reproach me and I reproach myself when I deny you the confidences you have the right to demand. To whom may one go if not to his mother when in trouble? Whom should one shield from the burden of his own worries if not his mother? There you are! Now take my problem. On one side a woman whom I sincerely love and admire, and whose companionship is so necessary to me that in spite of four different efforts to give her up in the past year, I have proven myself unable to do so. On the other, my family, who have always been near to my heart, and the promotion of whose happiness has been my life's ambition, but the bitterness of whose opposition has outrun my wildest expectations. One thing that has surprised me most, is that my admiration, based on intimate knowledge, instead of weighing in her favor has been cast in the account against her. You think that if I marry Nell Bassell I shall be unhappy. *You may be right.* I know that if I do not I shall be of all men most miserable. If I marry her, the issue of happiness or unhappiness will lie almost absolutely in her hands. I have confidence in her. I do know that in some way I must discharge myself of this load of raging discontent."

The controversy went on. The older sister Lillie wrote in her temperate and understanding way that John had talked to her about it a year before, that she was now sure that they were deeply in love, and thought they had better marry.

By summer John wrote his mother with greater exasperation. "I wanted to have you and Father believe that she is not the basely artful and designing creature you believe her, but only a woman who has both loved and suffered much. I do not believe that you or Father or I are capable of either so greatly.

"For her divorce she had Biblical grounds, let the rule be believed in all of its rigidity (and I do not give assent to that). As for the slander, the stories are false, and should a man deny to the woman he loves the protection of his name?

"These are not the things that move me. Chiefly I regret the sorrow I have given her, you, and all concerned. Since I came to manhood I have given those nearest me so much more of sorrow than of joy—sorrow even to the grave itself—that I am doubly remorseful now. Forgive me, and I beg of you think more tenderly of her whose grief is greatest."

When Grandmother saw that the marriage was going to take place, she did her best to bridge the chasm. She sent for Nell and talked to her understandingly. She wrote announcing it to the McDonalds, and suggested that John would appreciate letters from them.

Their response was warm, immediate, and characteristic. No tendency to block the happiness of others could survive in that atmosphere. In her last illness my mother herself had found an opportunity to whisper, "Em, I do not think a man ought always to live alone." Consistently, Grandmother McDonald had expressed the wish that John might find companionship.

"With your experience and my own before me," he answered her, "I need no assurance of its joys, yet the proposition is frightfully complex."

Now they welcomed Nell so cordially that she conceived an affection for the whole family and visited them as often as she could stand the plumbing—which was not often.

John's confidence in Nell's care for his happiness was not misplaced. For the rest of her life his advantage and his comfort were her constant concern. It is not too much to say that his public career could not have taken place without her.

Once married, she did her best to be a good daughter- and sister-in-law. Relations were cordial, with a certain reserve on both sides, although she never did remove the ban on Nan. With me she made great efforts. She fashioned for me delicate and elaborate dresses, she tried to correct my posture, skin, and hair. She started me on a round of party-going.

So a third household, a third totally different approach to life was added to the two I had already known. One major point set it apart from the others. My stepmother was happier when I was not around. In spite of her determined kindness I could see this, and it came as a shock to one who had been "raised a pet." She readily subscribed to the theory—if she did not initiate it—that I should not be uprooted, but should stay with my two sets of grandparents as usual, and visit Washington only for the short vacations.

On the surface all was bright. After several years, she asked me to stop calling her Miss Nellie. Never one for half measures, I said that I would call her Mother. Tears came into her eyes and she put her arms around me. "I want to be so much to you," she said.

It was true, but although we both tried we could not bring it off. We were too different. When our orbits touched we tangented time and again. She was a great beauty, and I was not—with the additional handicap of looking like my mother. She had not gone beyond the seventh grade because of an eye difficulty after scarlet fever, and she made fun of women who thought they had to have an education to get along. She gave me all her laughing worldly wisdom, and I did not know how to profit by it.

"John didn't marry me. I married him. A smart woman can get any man she likes. It is better to lie a little than to suffer much."

When I visited she insisted that I bring friends, she arranged entertainment for me, introduced me, tried to give me a good time. I enjoyed it, but what I really wanted was time with my busy father. This I could not have. For my part, I could see his happiness and I did not wish to obstruct it. I tried to conform, tried to make no demands which would be met with opposition. That had to suffice.

If at eleven I had had the understanding which years have brought, I might have won my stepmother over, but it is one of the strange conditions of life that often by the time we learn how to do something, the necessity for doing it has passed. Nowhere is this more true than in the troubled sphere of human relations.

Perhaps it was from the beginning inherently impossible for

us really to please each other. She was willing to share my father with his work and with the world, but not with any other individual whatsoever. Worse still, I was the living representative of a past which she wished to expunge. She could not bear to leave the two of us alone together. Fighting her own strong feelings all the time she deserves great credit for what she did for me. In her way she gave me much.

XI

When my father ran for Congress a second time, in 1912, he was justified in "running scared." "I shall be glad when my official life is over, but the idea of being beaten in the election is a whip of scorpions to me." He won by a narrow margin of only one hundred and sixty-nine votes.

With a beautiful and driving wife to push him, he was on his way to a wider field. The new Mrs. Davis was an excellent housekeeper and liked to exercise her skill. They soon moved from his bachelor rooms to an attractive apartment on Sixteenth Street. Endowed with gaiety and wonderful good looks, all rosy marble crowned with gold, Mother could make an impact on any social scene, and she did not waste her opportunity.

Soon they were giving dinner parties for the Vice-President or the Chief Justice. John would not have thought of it himself, or if he had would have been afraid to try it. The first effort was almost a disaster, for the hired waiters got drunk and had to be fired in the middle of the meal. Nell carried it off with the help of the parlormaid, who had already been found to be a necessary permanent fixture. The contretemps was only a minor dip in an ascending spiral.

They bought an electric, open as a buggy, in which Mrs. Davis, draped in a gauzy veil, called for her husband every evening at the Congressional office building. This vehicle, known as the Little Pet, had temperament. On hills all passengers except the driver were expected to get out and walk, and were lucky if they did not have to push. The batteries ran down at unexpected points all over the city, necessitating frantic calls to the garage. In rain we were protected only by the hood and a rubber apron.

Before the end of his second term in Congress, Father was appointed Solicitor General. Then the electric had to be exchanged for a more elegant model, a high glass box in which the occupants sat as if ready for a game of cards.

Mother had a slogan: "A man in your position." "A man in your position ought to have a better car . . . somebody between me and the stove . . . a parlormaid to do the things for your clothes I have been doing . . . a mending woman to make things last longer."

"If I had ever had enough money," Father used to say, "I should have been too lazy to be fit for cat bait."

For the first time in his life he was really comfortable, his suits brushed and pressed at home, his meals excellent and regular. Casual hours for eating did not suit Mrs. Davis. If he were late, she sputtered like a skyrocket and protested with tears that she could not make a proper home for him under such conditions. He believed her and complied. From then on they dined at seven, not five to seven, or seven ten. They began to collect their furniture, avoiding the Victorian style which lay heavy in their backgrounds. After a brief flirtation with the shiny mahogany of the period, taste came to rest on Chippendale.

Thriving under the new management, John put on so much weight that he could no longer be called "Bones," and wrote home letters defensively happy. Nell had made the apartment so attractive. It was restful to come home in the evening and sit by his own fireside. Nell was rolling bandages for the Red Cross. Nell was much in demand. As he settled into his new life, he took on a lighthearted and humorous tone missing since his youth.

Then and always he found it easy to entrust the details of living to his wife. In the first place, she was efficient. In the second place, he liked to leave argument in the courtroom and live in domestic peace. In the third place, he enjoyed seeing her happy, and she was not happy when crossed. In the fourth place, and of supreme importance, this method left him free to work.

The Davises soon had more invitations than they could handle, and proud though John was of Nell's success, he protested. He had always made friends of those with whom he worked, whether chief justices, colleagues, secretaries, or toiling young law clerks, "my spiritual sons"; but he was too much like his mother to care for formal entertaining. "Life is too short to waste in the society of people who bore one." The "dyspeptic rhinoceros" to which he had compared himself had been driven underground, but still gave forth an occasional grumble.

Just before he was appointed Solicitor General, he had made the only effort of his life to obtain a position—a seat on the bench of the United States Circuit Court for the Fourth Judicial District. When President Wilson gave the judgeship to a friend, John Davis was through with such attempts forever, and annoyed with himself for having tried.

Soon after, Nell sat next to the President at dinner, and in the course of conversation he absent-mindedly told her of the pleasure it had given him to appoint a friend met on a cruise to a recent vacancy on the bench.

She looked at him. "I have heard of Judge Wood."

Suddenly Wilson remembered. "Oh my God!"

They had a good laugh, and the President carried away an impression of charm which did not harm John's future. Of importance to the future also was the fact that Mrs. Davis formed a close friendship with Mrs. Robert Lansing, whose husband was then counselor of the State Department. Through their wives, Father and Lansing became friends.

During these years in Washington, I was a spectator rather than a participant. I enjoyed the clean wide city and the excitements it offered, but I sometimes felt uncomfortably like the third person on a honeymoon; as in fact I was.

Nevertheless, on my brief, infrequent visits history unrolled before me. We were sitting one night at dinner when we heard the newsboys calling "extra!" in the darkened streets, as was the custom in those days before the radio. Father hurried down to buy a paper and came back gravely, carrying the story of the *Titanic.*

In April 1917, I heard President Wilson read to the joint Houses of Congress his message asking for a declaration of war with Germany. The representatives and senators, packed into the larger Chamber, applauded wildly when he finished, except for Miss Jeannette Rankin, the first congresswoman, who wept, openly and uncontrollably, and Senator Robert La Follette, his arms ostentatiously folded, his back against the wall, scowling.

An experience need not be historic to be memorable. With a friend I was taken to visit the commandant at Annapolis, where godlike first classmen were ordered to entertain us. Under the eye of the admiral discipline made them conceal their horror at dragging two girls barely in their teens to the Christmas hop. In a charming house on the outskirts of the city, I attended a tea dance on a *Sunday*. After a brief struggle with conscience, the many-time loser, I danced, was not struck by lightning, and continued the practice with a comfortable mind.

Amid these pleasures, improvement was not neglected. Efforts were made to have me taught to play tennis (useless), to speak French (more hopeful), to correct my posture by a brace which I removed as soon as I got away, and to dress fashionably (this I enjoyed).

With one thing and another, I was satisfied to have Father live indefinitely in Washington, but it was not to be.

Within his new happiness, and above his diversions, his work went on untiringly, unremittingly, increasing in interest and importance. Nothing interfered with that, and nothing prevented his writing about it, two or three times a week, either to his father or his mother. To his father he wrote as to a senior partner who would be interested; to his mother as to the temperament most akin to his own. (Not that he had ever wished to marry her like.) When he started as Solicitor General, he threw his usual terrors on her.

"I write September 14th with a positive shudder, for it means that October 14th and the opening of the Supreme Court are but thirty days away. No schoolboy ever dreaded his commencement day oration more. As the work of this position opens up to me, and my own slender equipment becomes more evident, I have a positively smothering sense of my inadequacy, more than I have ever been sensible of before, and closely bordering on panic. I am conscious of the fact that I am letting my fears oppress me beyond reason, yet try as I will I cannot shake them off. Yesterday afternoon I threw down my books in disgust, telephoned for a horse, and took to the open fields for a couple of hours. It helped some, and it may be that more of the same will minister to my mind, well nigh diseased along the line I mention."

The day drew inexorably closer, was met, and passed. By November he could write for the same comprehending eye, "You can imagine that I am in happier frame this day than I was a week ago when my Supreme Court cases were still ahead of me. I wrote Father that I had come off alive, and of course there have been those who made the customary comment which every speaker good or bad is sure to receive. I am conscious that I did not do myself full justice, largely on account of my nervousness. I can do better, and so help me I will before they are done with me."

His anxieties, which were real enough, struck Nell as amusing aberrations. "John works *terribly* hard," she said, commiseratingly, and never quite grasped the fact that he enjoyed it. When he quaked she made the right responses, with an absent mind, and suggested a good two-handed game as a diversion. Bezique was a favorite. "John likes to get away from his work when he comes home."

Without such relaxation he could hardly have stood the pace. "I began work a little after eight in the morning and stopped at midnight, with allowance for meals. How's that for the defender of the eight-hour law?

"If a lawyer made as many mistakes as those of other professions do, he would not last long. While I disappointed myself, Senator —— disappointed me also. He knew of his case only what he read in the brief his colleagues had written, made much of his argument with his nose between the leaves of his brief. Again I repeat that there is little difference in lawyers save in industry, and a great name is a poor substitute for the latter."

John did not intend to fail in industry. Through all the changes in his life, his basic purpose drove a straight furrow. He went to work on the International Harvester case, an appeal by a company about to be dissolved as a monopoly in restraint of trade.

"I must cut out diversion until I see daylight ahead. This record has been reduced under the rule to narrative form, and consists of 1500 closely printed pages. It makes desperately slow reading, and I am not one third of the way through. When I have the facts in mind, I shall turn to the task of analysing all the leading Anti-Trust decisions to fasten my grip on the law. The case will be argued for the Harvester Co. by John P. Wilson, head of the Chicago bar, and Frank B. Kellogg of Minneapolis. I want to strain the last trace chain."

In the end, his grip on the law firmly fastened, he was able to write his father: "This was a great day for us in court, the Government winning in seven out of ten cases. (And the three we lost I had urged the Government not to appeal.) One of the wins was in the Montana Oil case—Taft's withdrawal order. Justice Day delivered the dissenting opinion and afterward sent me a pencilled note—'And *you*, a Jeffersonian Democrat, have done this thing!' I should have answered him that it was due to the necessity of defending Republican presidents."

The Solicitor General could feel by now that his tools were shaping to his hand. He was still using fifty minutes of his allotted hour and a half for argument, but had the satisfaction of seeing the justices rouse from their somnolence and listen when he spoke. Justice Day was heard to refer to him as "the most deludering man I know." John G. Johnson of Philadelphia, in opposition, called him "one of the most concise speakers at the bar, and one of the most dangerous." President Wilson summoned him back to Washington from a vacation, "because we are in need of the best advice obtainable." Chief Justice White treated him like a son.

He and White used to take long walks together, while the older man told how he had gone into the Confederate army in Louisiana when only twelve, and how his formal education ended then. As a result, he was ear rather than eye minded, and had to read briefs aloud to himself in his chambers to be sure that he had grasped them. Once, speaking of the Civil War, he paused on a Washington street corner to exclaim, "My God, sir, how terrible if we had won!"

Back in Clarksburg, John's mother, increasingly frail, rocked by her gas fire or tended her garden against the doctor's orders, and lived on her son's letters. When he wrote, "Am still loading my guns," or "I want to give it the best that is in me," she knew that he had learned what she had tried to teach him. She could afford to overlook the occasional rebellion. "Hang the Sherman law, its framers, evaders, interpreters, all in short save its toiling defenders, of whom I am humbly which." It did not concern her to wonder where this new life of John's might take him. She had always spurred him to do his best and leave the rest to fate. She could count herself satisfied and even cautiously admit some pride.

When Grandfather died in the spring of 1916, all her children rallied to show her their devotion. In that time of deep sorrow, her son sustained her in the way which helped her most, by going on with his work as she meant him to do.

"I wish I could be in two places at once," he wrote. "Here at my work, and with you in Clarksburg. To feel that you need me, and that I could if I were there relieve you of many of your problems and cares, makes me ill content indeed.

"I shall do all I can, but that will be far too little, nor shall I ever under any circumstances be able to do for you all that you deserve, or all that my heart desires.

"Thank God for a life filled with work and responsibility. I have moments when I allow myself the luxury of grunting and bemoaning, but down in my soul I know at the time that it is all play-acting, and that I could not exist in idleness."

His mother could understand this point of view, since it was she who had trained him in it, and she drew a profound solace from his acceptance of it. He was not only her heart's core, her support, both spiritual and material, but in a real sense which he was quick to admit, he was her achievement. It was a favorite theory of my stepmother's that the Davises were cold and unemotional. I cannot imagine how this notion could survive when all of them quivered with feeling, the stronger for being infrequently expressed; when the atmosphere among them was one of love intense to the point of discomfort, and, it must be admitted, not infrequently lit by the flames of disagreement in matters of opinion.

On his fortieth birthday my father wrote to my grandmother a letter which would crown any mother's life.

"With the exception of my thirtieth birthday, which I signalized by horse-whipping Wilbur Morrison, I have nothing by which to mark my milestones. But to have you say that after forty years you are still proud of me, is praise enough. If ever any man was the work of another's hand, I am of yours, and the mental habits you rubbed into me in my first ten years of life, went too deep for alteration. In temperament and disposition too, we are entirely too much alike for either of us to criticize the other safely. (They did all the time.) I should like to think that in my forty years I had put no extra gray hairs in your head, and I deeply trust that in the years to come I can help to smooth the few wrinkles that have gathered beneath them. As I look back over the forty years that are past, and realize that I have come more than half the way, I do not have any sense of satisfaction, but feel rather that the last words of Cecil Rhodes apply: 'So much to do, so little done'."

The reference to Wilbur Morrison may be parenthetically explained. He was editor of the Republican paper in Clarksburg, and in the spring of 1903 he undertook to cast doubt on the veracity of John J. Davis. John W. bought a new buggy whip, hunted for Morrison, met him on the street, informed him of what was coming, and proceeded to beat him heartily until he ran up the steps of his office, falling, they say, at the first try. Then John walked over to the courthouse and asked to be fined for assault and battery.

John W. had a temper and his mother knew it. In his childhood she had written during a visit from a little cousin, "Johnny is a little rough for our John. I am scared to death all the time that he will make John W. mad, and then Johnny will find that he has been playing with fire."

But this was Washington, and the days of personal encounter had ended, the atmosphere was urbane and benign—although not to the point of suffering fools gladly.

"I read Senator G on canal tolls, and—most unexpectedly—his flag, my flag, thy flag, her flag, its flag, our flag, your flag, and their flag, indivisible, indestructible, inevitable, and interminable. The truth is that G. is not and never has been a real lawyer, but a peewee and a shark by nature, with limelightis in its most Chatauquaed form, and for that disease there is neither amelioration nor cure."

Fears, sorrows, worry, success, jokes; to this mother all could be confided. Yet their close and loving association caused no loss of freedom, for she cared too deeply about the right of making up her own mind ever to infringe on that privilege in another. Only relentless time ended their deepening friendship.

In the spring of 1917 the letters ceased. There were never to be any quite like them again. During his long life, Father carried on a wide correspondence: devoted letters, humorous letters, letters in verse, important letters, but never again the unabashed mirror of the heart and mind that had been revealed to Julia McDonald and Anna Kennedy.

He called me at the Shipley School, where I was studying. Always terse and dry on the telephone, this time he had not a word to spare.

"Julia, it is over. Your grandmother died this morning."

I could not answer. I had known that she was ill, that she was at Johns Hopkins. I could not imagine life without her.

"Did you hear me, Julia?"

"Yes," I said.

He told me what train I should catch that evening. "We will all be on it."

Still I had nothing to say.

"Do you understand?" he asked, and I heard his voice break.

"I understand," I said, and we hung up.

After the funeral I heard my father talking with Aunt Emma in the library. "We are on the firing line now, Em."

He marched back to Washington to confront whatever responsibilities life might bring him. Although that penetrating and astringent spirit could no longer delight us with her pithy comments and her responsiveness to our interests, she could not be forgotten. To those whom she had unflaggingly instructed, her clear mind, her crystalline integrity, and her mental energy could not be wholly lost.

XII

Forty-five, and five years Solicitor General, my father was growing restless. He felt that he had spent too much time in what he called "*temporary* situations," which did not permit him to build any security for his family. In his ten years of private practice he had accumulated only modest savings, and had severed all outside interests while he held office. Although he enjoyed his work as Solicitor General, he thought he could not afford to go on with it. "I would go far to find a more congenial office, but I am determined to go *up*, or *out*, but not *on*."

After the United States entered World War I, however, he

would not resign. A man in his forties, notably unmilitary in temperament, could render his country no better service. Remaining in Washington, he joined the group of cabinet members who drilled and exercised every morning under the eye of Walter Camp. It was a sacrificial gesture on the part of John Davis, who hated exercise, although perhaps it did not daunt the Kaiser.

In August 1918, much to his surprise, Father was sent to Berne as one of the special diplomatic commissioners, to negotiate an agreement for the treatment and exchange of prisoners of war. He welcomed the chance to move closer to what was going on.

When he arrived at Liverpool, after a crossing on a blacked-out ship, he was told that Ambassador Page had resigned from the London embassy because of ill-health. He felt decently regretful, but not involved, until in London he had the shock of his life. The chairman of his commission, J. W. Garrett, then Minister to Holland, handed him a confidential telegram from Robert Lansing, who had become Secretary of State.

"Will you accept the Ambassadorship to the Court of St. James? This offer is made after consultation with Attorney General Gregory, who though feeling deeply that he cannot fill your place, has given his unqualified approval. . . . Please do not telegraph to Mrs. Davis, as the matter must be kept entirely secret. The State Department will communicate to her anything you care to say."

Knowing her John, Nell had sent a message of her own. "Insist you accept regardless of personal interests or sacrifice. You must not decline."

Cut off from anyone with whom he could talk the matter over, John exploded in the diary he kept of the trip. "I could not have been more surprised if the dome of St. Paul's had fallen on my head, and I so expressed myself to Christian Herter, of whom I had to make a confidant in order that he might code my reply."

The reply was characteristic. He doubted his fitness for the post. He did not have the money to carry it. He wished to have Nell asked to consider how it might affect Julia's whereabouts and education.

"Your fitness beyond question," Lansing answered. As for the rest, the post would cost about thirty-five thousand dollars a year, and the salary was seventeen thousand, but it need be held for only two years. John could draw on his principal, "a procedure which your wife approves," or he could borrow from intimate friends, "which I can arrange on terms which will in no way embarrass you or us."

The perplexed John Davis went on to Paris, where he obtained permission to confer with Ambassador Sharp, although the second telegram "did little to quiet my grave apprehensions as to the task itself."

"Diplomacy is not an occult science," Sharp said encouragingly. He was spending about forty-five thousand in Paris. He delivered a telegram from Mother saying that she *had* thought about Julia and *still* insisted that John must accept. She was fuming in Washington, knowing him capable of refusing, and unable to reach him with the splendid arguments which were chasing through her head. If at this point she had received the agitated letters her husband sent through the diplomatic pouch, she would have been even more disturbed.

September 7

Dear Lover

Nothing could show me more clearly my utter dependence on you than the despondency I feel in having to wrestle with such a problem without having you at hand to talk it over. I confess that the prospect frightens me more than it lures me. Am I fit for that sort of work? Anything a lawyer is called upon to do I will attempt, but an Ambassador is supposed to be the eyes and ears as well as the tongue for his Government, and you know I am both an indifferent as well as an uncommunicative beast, who likes to go his own way on his own affairs and let others do the same and be damned to them. . . .

To resume my rumination. I am totally unused to diplomacy, but the mere formalities I suppose I could learn. The salary is but $17,000, expenses twice as much. Tossing in everything we have, we could not last long at that clip. You know my views of wealth. I do not care to be wealthy, but no amount of tinselled honor could compensate for a penniless old age. . . . I dread too a long separation from America. In fact I am homesick for it (and you) right now.

It is by far the gravest decision of my life, and here I am to muscle it out without your courage to bolster me. I could almost wish it had not been offered, for I am asked now to put all I have on the table and risk it on a single throw. . . . The Solicitor Generalship is a quiet and sequestered harbor, this is the rough and open sea. I tell you, if I must work for the Government and not on my own, I am much more decently equipped to be a judge than a diplomat.

What about Julia? I would hate to interrupt her course at Wellesley, and yet after all the days of her life I have already lost, I *cannot bear* the thought of putting the ocean between us. Neither can I risk on a mad gallop after fame, the funds from which she must be educated.

What a life I have had in my small way, hankering always for the Bar, and dragged from it again and again, and always without much premonition. So it goes. This is good night.

Your distressed
John.

Four days later he had sufficiently recovered to wire his acceptance before he left for Berne, but he was still disturbed.

How *can* I do it? But what an opportunity! Things have come to a pretty pass when a man's best friend, his wife, his best friend's wife, his official chief, his President, all unite to do a thing like this to him when he is three thousand miles away from home and defenceless.

The physical danger of the air raids in Paris did not cause him nearly so much agitation. At the first alarm, "after a leisurely toilet," he went out in the porte-cochere of the hotel to see what was going on. At the second, he joined his fellow guests in the cellar. At the third, he decided to stay in bed and get some sleep.

His cable of acceptance was not answered, and his next news of his post was an announcement in the Paris *Herald* on September 18th. He wired Lansing again, "intimating some natural curiosity as to my exact status."

Lansing replied that he had made the announcement in a hurry because the news was beginning to leak out. Davis was to finish in Berne, and then should have a month in America "to become familiar with the pending questions with Great Britain." A note of encouragement was added. "In all my experience I have never known so unanimous a voice of approval by press and people as your appointment has called forth. You would have been most gratified if you were here."

Looking over the press clippings which reached him in Europe some weeks later, John Davis glumly concluded that Lansing had not read widely on the subject.

"Davis!" exclaimed the New York *New Weekly*. "When we consider that it might have happened to statesmen we know a lot about, Mr. Davis' anonymity is an asset for which we may well emit a sigh of relief. Let us not criticize, but shudderingly bear in mind the perils from which we have escaped."

The careful New York *Times* remarked, "The President has given the country another surprise." The *Tribune* was not so restrained. "A disappointing appointment. The President was not driven to such extremity." The New York *Post* chimed in.

"An able man, but Wilson has in our opinion made a mistake. A more distinguished man would have been better, not a personal favorite."

Current Opinion tried to see the brighter side. "Our new Ambassador is an intellectual prodigy, but is John W. Davis well enough advertized for the post?"

The subject of these observations rallied to go forward. At least he began to write more cheerfully to his wife.

> I am glad you and Julia bear up under the thought of London. You at least are adequate to the duties of your position. . . . How could I hope to get through without you? I do not intend to pretend to be anything other than I am—an American citizen of modest means, living like a gentleman, i.e. neither meanly nor extravagantly, doing his best to bear himself with the dignity befitting his office, but putting on no side; not taking himself too seriously, but realizing that he has a tremendous job on his hands and giving it all the steam in the boiler.
>
> As I see it the job must be handled by the entire firm of Davis, Davis, and Davis, and there is room for the junior partner.

In Berne, negotiations dragged. The enemy commissions, staying in the same hotel, were forced to stare through each other in the lobby or the dining room. Around the conference table they communicated through a Swiss interpreter, since they must not speak directly. Most of the work was done within the commissions themselves, where, as Davis put it, each phrase was argued as if they were in a debating society. The French were obstructive. In all the committee rooms, around all the tables of that era, the French were obstructive. They had one object, one interest: France. The Americans, making their first groping attempts at constructing a new world order, became exasperated. So did the British, playing their hand concealed as usual.

The niggling methods of negotiation, the snail's pace, were

a trial to Father, ever a man who liked to get things done, and now impatient to go home and settle his affairs. As October ended, the German attitude underwent a change. Their delegation made a quick dash to Berlin, returned with a mollified tone, and agreement was reached. Now it became a race to get the document printed for signing before the end of the war. On November 11, 1918, only a few hours before the armistice, the commissioners set their names to the papers, and John Davis was free to go home. By the armistice a general amnesty was ordered for all prisoners. "*Vale*, our agreement."

He shipped from Bordeaux as quickly as he could. Mother and I met him in New York on November 27 and greeted him with the news that he was to sail back on December 3 with President Wilson and our delegation to the Peace Conference. The new ambassador would not have a month to turn over his work to a successor, arrange his finances, and brief himself on his duties. He would have five days.

Like my father, I was still dazed and unbelieving. Wellesley had been remote from what was suddenly the stir of the great world. The excitement had indeed backwashed up there in the unpleasant form of an interview with me printed in the Boston *Post*. This revolting piece led off, "Eyes are the windows of the soul," and gave me a hard life among my college mates. "How," they would ask with sinister smirks, "is the dainty daughter of the dignified diplomat today?" Or, still quoting, "It must be the aboriginal Indian in you that drives you to the bow and arrow." (I had gone out for the undistinguished sport of archery because of a constitutional inability to hit or catch a ball.) The suffering caused by that reporter's lively imagination is far behind me now, but I can still remember the fire of it. I discovered the clipping among old papers last year and found it as painful as ever.

Arriving in Washington on special leave from college to welcome and wave farewell to my now noted father, I created a prodigy of interference. Mother, with her usual efficiency, had sublet the apartment as of December first, dismissed the servants as of that date, and ordered the moving van for the day before. All that was to go to England had been packed, the rest was disposed of or ready to be put in storage. I woke up on the morning of November 28 with badly swollen jaws. MUMPS.

It was thought at first that I could go to a hospital, but only the contagious hospital would have me. Since it was full of scarlet fever and meningitis, my father said flatly that I could not go. I could not be quietly removed in an automobile. Quarantine in those days lasted two weeks, and we were currently in the public eye, which as I came to learn, is as all-seeing as the eye of God. Incidentally, neither could I see my father, for he had never had mumps and could not risk them at this point. He called to me cheerily through my closed door on his way out each morning. Mother, who had had mumps, popped in from time to time to give me word on the disposal of Julia. In this family crisis, as in most others, there was eventually only one thing to do. Send for Aunt Em.

Father, of course, was busy to frenzy. When he called on his predecessor, Walter Hines Page, in St. Luke's hospital, he was told, "England is the most beautiful place in the world, but they pay for it by leading amphibious lives. Those people live like frogs." Many farewells had to be made, and the Chief Justice mournfully said that he had hoped to see Davis his successor on the bench. "I have had no better friend," John wrote, deeply touched.

One day could be given to clearing out his office, one day to his private affairs with his junior partner, Bryan Templeman, who came on from Clarksburg, and to arranging some financing through a Washington bank. He took the oath of his new office and spent one day in learning something about it. On that night he and Mother boarded the Presidential special for the trip to Hoboken, from which port they sailed on the *George Washington.*

Aunt Emma and I camped in the two rooms left furnished for us, while the tenants had to be put up at a hotel. For ten days after my parents had departed in glory with the great of America, we sat it out. There were no farewells for me, no hanging on the fringe of important events. To make it worse, after the first day I did not even feel ill.

XIII

Surprisingly enough, my father began his work in London before my cousin and I arrived to help him the following June. Katharine Watson, who preferred to be called Katy, was my stepmother's niece, two years younger than I, who sailed clutching a teddy bear, soon to be abandoned. With no friction between us, we led a subembassy life full of incident and interest, observing the world around us with a woodchuck's eye, insignificant but intent.

Handicapped though they were by our absence, it must be admitted that the new ambassador and his wife managed well during their first six months. John Davis claimed to be "giving an imitation of a young man scared to death," but he concealed it from the British.

When the Davises landed on December 14, "with a first experience of being piped over the side," they had already a few friends in London. Arthur Glasgow lent them his house on

Berkeley Square. The Earl and Countess of Reading had become intimates while at the embassy in Washington. On their second evening, the Davises dined with the Readings and found there only one other guest, Lloyd George. It was an excellent way of getting on easy terms with the prime minister. Conversation turned on whether or not the Kaiser should be tried as a war criminal. Davis and Reading thought not. Lloyd George, with his flair for the dramatic, was captivated by the possibilities of such a trial.

Father had already faced his first crisis when he discovered that he must wear a frock coat when he presented his credentials to King George V. The embassy staff, world-weary but efficient, arranged to have a tailor produce one within twenty-four hours.

Guided by the same experienced staff, Mr. Davis threaded the maze of protocol. He visited the ambassadors who outranked him in length of service at the post, he let the ministers visit him. He called ceremonially on the older members of the royal family, offspring and in-laws of prolific Queen Victoria, some of whom in thick German accents made a point of denouncing the Germans. He was amused when having written one letter according to instruction, beginning "Madame," and closing "Your Royal Highness's most obedient humble servant," he had a reply, "Dear Davis," signed "Beatrice."

Mother engaged a secretary and quickly took her department in hand. Lunches and dinners were accepted daily at first, in getting to know the people and the feel of the place. "The struggle of the Pilgrims and the American Society for the possession of my body on Washington's Birthday was solved by dates set for both." The members of the coalition government were met and also statesmen such as Asquith, out of power, but hoping to come in again. Speechmaking began.

The Davises had only two weeks to settle in and get acquainted before President Wilson arrived for his visit to the King. During that brief but golden interlude in time, everyone loved Americans. The visit progressed triumphally, flowers and cheers everywhere.

For the splendor of the King's banquet the royal gold plate was brought up from Windsor, where it had lain in safekeeping during the war. The new ambassador sat between Viscountess Chinda, wife of the Japanese envoy, to whom he found himself ceremonially married all winter by order of precedence, and Princess Pat, the King's first cousin. Since Viscountess Chinda had little English, and Mr. Davis no Japanese and poor French, their relationship had to be limited largely to cordial smiles and bows. The princess told him that she was announcing her engagement to a commoner next day and renouncing her royal rank. Her beautiful blue eyes sparkled with pioneering excitement over this daring and unusual step. She would not make a glorified butler of her husband, she said, and besides, she was sick of opening bazaars.

The King made a gracious speech, and the President responded, although not, his ambassador thought, with sufficient praise for England's part during the war.

The whirl of entertainment lasted four days: the prime minister's lunch, the President and Mr. Davis alone for dinner at the palace while Mrs. Davis gave a dinner for Mrs. Wilson at the embassy, a trip to the countryside, a second, but this time informal, dinner at the palace, where Mr. Davis sat next to the Queen, and found her easy to talk to. Then the President departed, leaving the course of history unchanged, but well satisfied with his reception. The ambassador mopped his brow and took a day to go over chancery matters with his Counselor, Butler Wright.

In that December of 1918, the peoples of the world, released from an intolerable burden, gazed at the lightened sky like sailors who had ridden out a typhoon, and indulged in the hope that no such storm could ever come again. Feeling the first joy of deliverance, the survivors forgot the grueling routine of keeping the ship afloat, and staring at each other with surprise and exaltation, felt for the moment no differences between them. For a moment, for one brief pause in history, they had a vision of a life in which all men agreed and lived as brothers.

At the end of the war to end wars, the American ambassador found it easy to talk of Anglo-American friendship. Woodrow Wilson, a universal hero, intended to lay the foundation of a permanent peace in Paris, with liberty and justice for all. Our gallant allies, carried away by enthusiasm, were even heard to say that our entrance into the war had turned the tide against disaster. Later on, when we said the same thing, they naturally resented it. The suggestion came better from them than from us.

Optimists could believe that the rainbow would never fade. Rudyard Kipling, a pessimist, bet Father that anti-American propaganda would start within three months and won with a comfortable margin. Kipling pointed out that the distrust was not one-sided. He had asked an American soldier in France how he liked Europe. The answer was prompt and forthright. "It is just as bad as Grandma said it was."

With ungrateful rapidity, the world forgot deliverance and drifted into the doldrums of peace. In Britain, labor troubles and the Irish question loomed. Winston Churchill, then secretary of war, launched an unsuccessful expedition against the Bolsheviks on the Archangel front, which his colleagues sourly called "his Russian adventure." An American sergeant, passing through London on his way home, had a long and bitter talk with his ambassador. The American troops in Russia did not know what they were supposed to be doing there. His captain had summed it up, reading a burial service over a dead comrade: "He died in a great cause, but we do not know what it is."

The British viewed with alarm the rise of American sea power, and Mr. Davis had to parry embarrassing questions on the subject. "Although I am not content with the way I came out of this brush, it will do me good when the next one comes."

In January, he was surprised to be summoned to Paris for advice and consultation, and also surprised at the conflicts he found there, even within the American delegation. Many complained that Wilson was risking all by attempting to do everything himself, while others firmly asserted that he alone could dominate the conference and achieve his hope. Davis made a report in the matter of the International Mercantile Marine, was unofficially offered the task of editing the Covenant of the League of Nations, unofficially declined—although he found it "crude and needing considerable condensation"—and thankfully returned to London.

By now he felt more at home there, and could speak "with more ease to myself" on the community of interest between the English-speaking countries. That spring he could write, "I have spoken some forty times on the same subject, and even to myself my voice gives out a hollow sound. It is wearisome to ring the changes on the same unvaried tune." Neverthless, he seemed to be satisfying both press and public. Once in a while, he escaped to the lawyers at the Middle Temple, where he had been made a bencher, and had "a grand evening."

Mother was in her element, house hunting, collecting a staff of sixteen servants, managing the busy social life. When the King's youngest son, John, died and the court went into mourning for a month, she liked the drama of having to wear black, even though it meant getting new clothes. She found a house on Chesham Place, belonging to Margaret, Lady Waterlow, who accepted the offer of fifteen hundred pounds a year—then about seven thousand dollars—plus rates and taxes. It was not a mansion, and Belgravia was not so fashionable as Mayfair, but it would have to do. Fortunately Mr. Glasgow's hospitality held out until the Davises could get possession.

John wrote to his law partner in West Virginia, "Dig up more money. It will take considerable financing to float so impecunious a person as myself for long on this sea." Sometimes he felt depressed, "too many dinners, too much wine, too little vigorous work."

He was seeing the last effort of London society to return to its prewar life; a life which had been the most comfortable, luxurious, and splendid in Europe; a life which after this brief rebirth, ended forever. Parliament opened in a blaze of uniforms and jewels, the first full-dress occasion since 1914. To be elegant enough, Mother borrowed Lady Reading's sables. Lloyd George made a speech which Father described as "politically adroit."

Carrying a cold caught in a London fog, the ambassador went again to France, this time to tour the battlefields with some generals. Again he was asked to comment on the Covenant of the League of Nations. He said bluntly that the idea of not submitting it to the Senate was "the worst of tactical errors."

In his diary he commented on his forty-sixth birthday, which had passed without celebration. "This year finds me again in what seems a temporary phase, and wondering as usual what the next turn of the wheel will produce. I earnestly hope that at least within the next twelve months I can take on a more stable form of existence."

The move to Chesham Place in May was made with the sense of urgency which had begun to seem normal to the Davises, for only two days after getting in, Mother, equal to any emergency, gave a dinner of twenty-five for Secretary of the Navy Daniels. Notable Americans came over in droves that spring to see how the face of the world still looked, and many of them made public comments which their ambassador had trouble explaining away.

Glumly he noted: "The outlook in Europe, with half a dozen little wars going on, forbids optimism. Clearly we are a long way from signing a treaty." He was congratulating himself on not being "in the mephitic air of Paris," when a telephone call summoned him to go there that night if possible, and next day without fail.

"Why I did not know. On arrival I found that I was there for service on the committee to draw up a scheme for the government of the occupied provinces, which Lansing cheerfully predicts may take three weeks." He had to stay for six.

The Four—Wilson, Lloyd George, Clemenceau, and Orlando—had been horrified at the draft submitted by the military and had determined to create a civilian control. The planning committee went to work, but at every meeting Maréchal Foch, one of the two members for France, ignored the instructions of The Four, objected to the whole idea, and insisted, as if presenting his point for the first time, that the *military* must control.

"Procrastination in Paris is certainly a fine art," Father commented. With all possible pushing, it was June 11 before the report could be signed and he could "escape to London."

There Ascot was upon him, and with it the Americans who wished to attend that famous royal race meeting. He wrote to Em, who had become his correspondent for home, "Here I sit parcelling out tickets to Ascot and presentations at Court among ambitious ladies, no more than ten percent of whom it is possible to gratify. It is more like settling postmasterships than anything I have done since I deserted that occupation, and gives just about as much general satisfaction."

In addition to the dining and the speaking, every weekend brought a country house party, which he now recognized as the best opportunity for discussing affairs with the leaders of Britain. Americans still felt that they should labor on Saturday, but in England the two-day weekend was firmly entrenched. Father discovered it for the first time in his life, and enjoyed it.

Although his wish to succeed drove him as hard as ever, at the end of six months his nervousness was gone. He knew now that he could get on with the British. He had made some real friends, who were to be his for life. In addition to this, the old brown city, that dowager among world capitals, had begun to work her spell upon him.

On June 30, Katy and I looked from our cabin porthole on the *Lapland*, saw the gray rain slashing at the gray stones of the Liverpool dock, felt the clammy chill.

We exchanged despairing looks. "Merry England!" we said.

Then my father came up the gangplank to meet us, and for me the sun came out.

XIV

"Now girls," Father said, standing in front of the empty grate in his study as if it could warm him, "you must not expect to live over here just as you did at home. The English do not give their daughters the freedom we do, and if you don't go by their rules they will think you are badly behaved. Remember that you are representing your country, and it will be judged by you."

He had been up since five that morning in order to meet us in Liverpool and had lunched with us on the boat train; now he was going to the chancery to catch up with the work of the day, yet he showed no sign of fatigue. He was wearing his family face, pink, gentle, calm, plainly glad to see us. When he looked like that we were willing to do anything to please him.

"For example," he continued, "you will have to be chaperoned going to and coming from parties. You may not dance in public places. You are always to go out together and never singly, even to shop or take a walk in the park. And neither of you is ever to go anywhere alone with a man, either by night or by day."

Katy and I looked at each other. Well! Put on the basis of patriotic duty, we gasped and agreed.

The first footman entered in his dark blue livery, with a red and white striped waistcoat and eagles on his buttons. "What will Your Excellency wear this evening?"

The ambassador groaned. "Full rig, William. The habiliments of joy."

Smiling no more than was correct, William hurried out. Benignly, Father continued to instruct us.

"The British are like Indians in their way of making friends. They look you over first. You will get along better if you always let them speak to you before you speak to them."

That was as much as he felt it necessary to tell us about the life we were going to lead, a change indeed from the easy comradeship of Indianapolis or of the Shenandoah Valley. On the next night, as complete strangers, we attended our first great ball—an ice bath.

We dined with Mrs. Waldorf Astor, not yet either a viscountess or the first woman member of Parliament. She took us on to the coming-out party of Lady Elizabeth Bowes-Lyon, a charming girl with violet eyes who was to become Queen of England, a fate no one suspected.

At the Astors', guests always had time to assemble before the hostess appeared. We were ushered without introduction into a room full of pretty girls swathed in tulle.

The house was 4 St. James's Square. The room was large, high, pale green, cold, and deathly quiet. Occasionally one of the girls murmured something to another in a tone of ennui and without changing expression. For all the attention paid to us, Katy and I might have been invisible. Since there were plenty of deep chairs and sofas, we sat down. After a while I could not bear it, and turning to the nearest girl, I ignored my father's instructions.

"What fun it is to go out to dinner in broad daylight at eight o'clock!"

"Really?" She neither looked at me nor altered her countenance. "I hate it."

The silence fell again. Unfortunately, I had spent my young life learning that to be successful a girl must chatter. In this nervous moment, balked at one point, I was irrepressibly compelled to try again.

"We landed only yesterday, but like all good Americans we went to the Tower of London this morning."

She did not turn her eyes from the wall at which she had been staring. "I loathe sight-seeing."

At dinner, I sat between a man who had lost his leg in the war, and a man who was announcing his engagement that evening and who spent the time toasting his fiancée across the table with longing eyes. Not much hope there for the dance to follow. Katy's position was equally unproductive.

The Earl of Strathmore had assembled a brilliant company for the launching of his daughter. With royalty present, all the men wore orders and decorations, all the women their most glittering jewels. Our own family were in view, having come on from another dinner, Mother shining in rose brocade, Father, as was prescribed for the American ambassador, the only man in the room with no medals on his plain black coat. It made him conspicuous. "Pure swank," Austen Chamberlain told him. We hailed them like sailors sighting land.

"It won't be necessary for us to stay," Father said, with a joy which he did nothing to conceal. "Mrs. Astor will see that you get home. Remember that you are not to leave alone."

Using a technique which he had brought to perfection, he talked cordially with some friends, registered his attendance, and faded into the night. A few minutes later, Mrs. Astor came up to us in the ballroom with a small lady in gray satin, wearing a diamond and pearl dog collar and a modest tiara.

"Good-by, you two," said the husky, unforgettable, Virginia voice. "I'm goin' now. Can't stand it another minute. This is Lady Edward Cecil, who will look after you."

Before we could gather our wits to say "take us," her tiny straight figure ran lightly down the stairs, train in one hand. With a way of making even a crown of huge diamonds seem casual, with a brusque wit frightening to the very young, she had scared us, but she had been something of home to cling to. Now we were abandoned to be as festive as we could.

Of course no one danced with us. We sat on the gold chairs and tried to look lively, sat on the stairs which were covered with young couples, went to that international refuge, the ladies room, came back, sat on the gold chairs and recited the alphabet to each other to keep our faces bright. Lady Strathmore made a conscientious effort to find us partners. She approached several exquisite guardsmen and addressed them earnestly. They looked over at us with startled expressions, deepening to horror, shook their heads firmly, darted away. Lady Elizabeth, the debutante, a small friendly girl with dark bangs, gave us the warm smile which has become famous, as she whirled past. She even brought one or two of her partners up to us.

"Howjudo," they murmured. "Sorry I'm engaged this dance."

The orchestra pounded away in a strict beat, the couples, both youthful and elderly, stalked about the room vaguely in time, leaning their heads away from each other, looking at the ceiling, rarely uttering a word, never committing the gaucherie of a smile. Could they possibly be as bored as they looked? I wondered. The only thing which kept us from despair was that a pool of tulle-shouldered, white-gloved girls shared our plight around the door with every dance. Plainly there were not enough men, and those who were there were not working at it.

At twelve I went to Lady Edward Cecil and hoped, with rather overdone politeness, that she would not let us keep her up.

"I have the most dissipated young daughter in London," she whooped. "I shan't be home until five this morning!"

I carried the news to Katharine, and we fell back again on the alphabet. The idea of a taxi wistfully occurred, but our word was out and we had to stay.

Another hour dragged on before Lady Edward Cecil swapped us off with Lord Broughton, a dear old boy who was chaperoning a granddaughter and longing for surcease. He took us home. We thanked him profusely. Safe inside our door we leaned together for strength, took off our shoes, and without a word crawled upstairs on all fours.

But depression could not last when there was so much of interest to see and do. By next morning we were as eager as ever. The youthful Miss Davis, who by now has lost all relationship to myself, stands exposed in the letters faithfully written to her aunts and faithfully preserved by them, as a creature of indestructible innocence and irrepressible bounce. Her enthusiasm played like a searchlight over everything, from family prayers with the canon of Westminster Abbey to punting on the Thames.

Our educational institutions (backed by family rigidity about improving the mind) had not released us in time for more than the last month of that London season. It was one of glorious gaiety for the initiates. For the first time in five years, the great houses were open, the jewels out of the vaults, the red carpets rolled down to the curbs. Everyone who had ever thought of giving a ball gave one that season.

The young men were still in uniform. The magnificent guardsmen had to sit with their legs stiffly stretched in front of them because their trousers were too tight to bend at the knee. The fliers, a new elite, called their D.F.C.'s the Distinguished Flirting Cross, and did their best to deserve them. The navy, like a wind from the sea, enlivened every party into which they rolled.

But the young men were in short supply. Cards came addressed to "Miss Davis and Partner," and an escort acted as a ticket of entry. Not only at our first dance, but at every dance the extra girls, trailing the inevitable tulle over the inevitable pastel dresses, huddled hopefully near the doors, trying to look happy. The dowagers, in their "glass hats," sat upright in the little rented gold chairs, watching through lorgnettes to discourage Daphne or Iris or Violet from dancing too often with some T.G.—some Temporary Gentleman, as the cruel phrase went, gentleman by grace of His Majesty's commission, whether wearing the Victoria Cross or not. In spite of them, the girls went on dancing with the Temporary Gentlemen. The Right Young Men, the young men who should have been there, were not, would never be there again. Hardly a distinguished family in England had not one son forever at rest in France; many had lost them all.

In any case the great London ball was not for the girls, and especially not for the debutantes, wretched young things, governess trained, paralysed with shyness, uncomfortable, dowdy, living through it as best they could. Unless they had had brothers, they and the opposite sex had been separated from the age of five, and now fate thrust them together with nothing to say to each other. Getting used to it took a bit of doing.

The balls were for the hardy who had survived the process, the successful older women, the ones who had made the right marriages and secured their places: for the beautiful Lady Curzon, an American, whose necklace of great diamond medallions hung below her waist, so heavy that the chain cut deeply into the back of her white neck—"I've married two women of the middle classes," Lord Curzon said; for the willowy Duchess of Sutherland, a shining column of white brocade; for the Marchioness of Londonderry in her crown of historic emeralds; for Mrs. Arthur Glasgow, redhaired and laughing; for Lady Diana Manners, already a legend. These had emerged from the dumpy chrysalis into an elegance and distinction and style unmatched in any country. Self-possessed, poised, chic, with the complexions of angels and a happy disregard of angelic behavior, the older women danced and flirted with all the men, and let the young girls either despair or learn to compete.

Taking as little part in the formal gaiety as he could, Father occupied himself during this time in making protests against increasing trade restrictions on American goods; in replying to inquiries from Lord Curzon, secretary for foreign affairs, as to whether the United States would take a mandate for Armenia, Batum, or Constantinople if British troops withdrew; in arranging for the Prince of Wales to visit the United States despite the noise Irish sympathizers were making there; and above all, and repeatedly, in trying to explain why America had not signed the treaty, and why the Senate was fighting the League of Nations.

Katy and I had little time to give to these questions; we were too busy seeing, feeling, meeting, learning. One of the first things we learned was that the house in Chesham Place, so grand at first sight, was not grand at all. Two or three balls were enough to shrink it down to size.

It had a pleasant small foyer with black and white marble tiles, a study, and a dining room on the first floor. Above, two drawing rooms opened into each other, with black marble pillars between, and a small room at the back for confidential teas. Father and Mother had their suite on the third floor—I must have been in it at least once, but cannot remember when—and Katy and I two bedrooms on the fourth. We needed all our bounce to get up those stairs. Like every house in London, the furniture consisted of English antiques, chintz-covered sofas, shelves after hanging shelves of figurines. I never saw the domestic offices in the basement, nor the servants' bedrooms on the fifth floor, and doubt if Mother did after she looked over the house for the first time. The cook and the butler brought her their books in the morning, and she dealt with everything through those august personages.

Katy and I soon found that Mrs. Findlatter, the cook, whom we would not have known had we met her on the street, was far too grand to cook for us when Their Excellencies were out. To a dinner party she gave an artist's care, creating miracles of molded salmon, grouse with breadcrumbs, soufflés, crèmes brulées, baked Alaskas. We were not often invited to these affairs, but often enough to recognize her skill. If alone for a meal, we fell into the hands of the kitchenmaids, or for all I know of the tweeny, and could expect dried chicken wings, brussels sprouts, and a gay finale of blancmange.

Mrs. Findlatter ate in her own sitting room with Carter, the black-clad butler of unassailable dignity, with Short, who was Mother's maid, and with Smith, the chauffeur. The four housemaids, two footmen, and Edith—maid to the young ladies and a blessing we had not expected—ate in the servants' hall. The two kitchen maids, the between-maid or tweeny, the odd man, and the boy had to be content with the kitchen. Carter, who ran the dining room and the footmen, had two distinguishing characteristics: he was never to be caught carrying anything and he lived out. I think the footmen lived out too, but can't be sure. It was fixed in the complicated mores that Findlatter and Short were entitled to have their morning tea brought in bed, just as the family did.

All of these people of necessity spent the greater part of their time in waiting on each other. The real work of the household devolved upon the tweeny, the boy, and the odd man, who lived in a hole in the basement, smelled of drink, and ran gaspingly about his work. This trio had no one to wait on them, and did everything that no one else wished to do, from morning teas and cans of hot water to boots and coal scuttles.

Short was a bustler; a cheery little body straight out of a Barrie play. She admitted no negative thinking whatever. On the dankest morning she drew the curtains with a glad cry, "It's a lovely day, Miss! Keeping fine!" which meant that fog or rain did not prevent seeing the other side of the street. As soon as I got to know her, I sent home for a copy of *Pollyanna, The Glad Book,* her kindred spirit. She adored it. She traveled with Mother to the weekend parties, and by virtue of ambassadorial rank sat at the right of the butler in the great houses, unless downgraded by some maid of visiting royalty.

Edith, our own white rabbit, stood in awe of her, of us, and of the world. We could never push her conversationally beyond "Yes, Miss" and "No, Miss." Like the housemaids, she scurried here and there, usually out of breath, and trying to be where we were not.

Fantastic era, when the goal of the head servants was to have the work accomplished so that the master and mistress need not be aware of it. Cook and butler had worked their own way up from tweeny and boy, and they treated their juniors with a rigid discipline which would never have been enforced from upstairs. The young ones bore it, sustained by the hope of being equally grand some day. The odd man was, in all probability, a boy who had not made good. All ran by magic, and we danced over their heads.

On our second day in London we heard the royal heralds proclaim the peace from the balcony of St. James's Palace, the treaty signed at last. The Prince of Wales, who was living there, had given us a special invitation. We went in a back door to avoid the crowd and were led by his equerry through the ancient crooked corridors, walked by centuries of kings. The heralds announce only peace or war, the death or the accession of a king. In their playing-card costumes, unchanged since the middle ages, they seemed to my eyes so straight out of *Alice in Wonderland* that I expected to see them blow around the courtyard at the end.

Our next event was the Fourth of July reception, which all heads of United States missions were expected to give to any Americans who cared to attend, invitations not necessary. It assembled some unusual characters.

"How do you do?" with a clank of jet beads. "I am the Countess —— from Cincinnati, Ohio. Have you read my latest book?"

"I am hoping to," Miss Davis parried.

Our minister to Finland breezed through the door, slipped on a small rug, fell flat on his back, rose undamaged, and passed out his calling cards to the receiving line.

An unsavory character in khaki kept asking us to "dance just once with the American uniform." Later we heard that he had gone to jail for impersonating a soldier.

A woman in a great hat of ostrich plumes and a lavender feather boa which cascaded over a plaid skirt and the surprise of white tennis shoes, came up the front stairs, went down the line, descended the rear stairs to the dining room, ate a good meal, got to the door, said she had forgotten her umbrella, went up the front stairs, went down the line, etc., etc. After observing several of these performances, Father detailed a third secretary to place her umbrella in her hand and guide her to the exit, for the time drew near when the family would like to sit down.

She was waiting for him at the chancery next morning. "Mr. Davis, you'll never guess where I spent last night. I had nowhere to stay, so I broke a window and they locked me up, but as soon as I got out I hurried around. I'm just as I was when I left your party, just as I was, but I wanted to tell you what a wonderful time I had!"

Murmuring something about keeping the prime minister waiting, the ambassador plunged past her. Care of one's nationals is a first duty, even when it extends to having them committed.

Always financially pushed, Father recorded that they had prepared for twelve hundred at the party, and he did not think more than six hundred came. Furthermore, he had been notified the day before that his meager entertainment allowance had been discontinued. We ate left-over aspic for weeks. However, "I was quite proud of the appearance of Julia and Katharine at their first big function, and Nell of course carried it off well."

Happily enough, not all the London balls proved like the first one. At another, the whole American army seemed to be crowding up the stairs, and when we saw the familiar uniform we did not wait to be introduced. General Pershing and his staff had come over to take part in the peace parade, and from the general down they were a joy to us. Soon we were really dancing, not merely walking around the floor. It had been our private notion that the young Briton did not know that the ankle was a joint.

We watched the parade from a balcony in Lowndes Square. The picked troops of each of the allies took long to pass: the Serbians, led by a small colonel with an unforgettable swagger; the Australians, with their free stride; but the Americans had the best of it, they were the tallest, the freshest, the strongest. They brought tears of pride to our eyes.

We closed the season on July 28 with a dance at Chesham Place for the Prince of Wales and his two brothers, Prince Albert and Prince Henry—and the *we* is purely editorial, for the efficient Mrs. Davis managed it singlehanded, as well as the dinner for forty which preceded it.

The princes were pleasant young men, small, slender, intensely shy. The P.O.W. in the days when those initials meant Prince of Wales and not prisoner of war was not permitted to dance with any unmarried girl except the daughter of his hostess. This duty performed, and it must happen only once, he was expected to amuse himself with the young married women, who were thought (how wrongly) to be safer. During dinner he said little, smiled the wistful boyish smile which made him the darling of the public, nervously rolled his bread into pellets which he arranged around his plate.

"The war has at least done one good thing," he told my father. "It has kept me from having to marry one of those damn German princesses."

Albert and Henry, who had not the succession to consider, were not so restricted, but Henry, now Duke of Gloucester, suffered such shyness that he would stand in front of a girl whom he intended to ask for a dance, unable to get a word past his paralysing stammer. Unless she had the wit to ignore etiquette and address him first, he might end by turning puce-colored and dashing away.

Prince Albert, whom no one then called George, who had not yet persuaded Elizabeth Bowes-Lyon to marry him, although it is said that he had loved her from the first time he saw her, who was not yet even Duke of York, never appeared to anyone, and especially not to himself, as the future King.

At our party he and I were waltzing between the two rooms when he caught his ankle on a guardsman's spur. He tottered, and I mistakenly tried to catch him. He fell flat on his back, and I on my hands and knees in the royal stomach.

I rolled off and sat stunned, watching three generals spring forward to pick up the prince, reassemble him, adjust the pale blue ribbon of the Garter across his chest. It was he who remembered me and helped me up. Solemnly we began to dance again, on the principle of getting back on the horse which has thrown you, and because we could not think what else to do. His Royal Highness was blushing furiously, and since he did not smile I could not.

"Should you mind if we sat this out?" he said at last.

"Of course not, Sir."

We found comparative privacy on the stairs, which were rather less full of young couples than usual. He rubbed his ankle. I expressed concern. He assured me that it was unnecessary. Then he looked at me and I looked at him, youth boiled up in us and we both roared with laughter. It was a relief, and the more we felt relieved, the more we laughed.

"One feels such an ass," he said.

We always had a cordial regard for each other after that, and he never failed to ask me to risk a dance.

By the end of that July Katy and I had been presented to the King and Queen at a Buckingham Palace garden party, the wartime substitute for a court, we had seen as many historic sights as we could assimilate, we had watched the boat races at Henley, been to Eton with beaux, met hundreds of personages, and found a few young people with whom we could be truly friendly. The balls terrified us no longer.

"If this is London we like it," we caroled.

Father noted the comment in his diary, adding indulgently, "Gloria juventatis."

XV

"Now that those dreadful balls are over we can begin to enjoy ourselves," Miss Davis wrote her Aunt Em.

"I'm through with boys, give me men," commented Miss Watson, her teddy bear deserted.

During August we all stayed with an American friend in the picture postcard town of Sonning-on-Thames, from which Father could commute daily. That is how we came to be there on St. Bartholomew's Day, the anniversary of the slaughter of the Innocents, the first and only time my father ever spoke to me in anger. Katy and I still exchange messages on the twenty-fourth of August.

There had been a coming and going of all ages during the weekend, and by Sunday night the juniors were reduced to two girls and one young man, dancing to the gramophone, while the older party played bridge in another room. The man was Sam Dickson, pink-cheeked, rotund, third secretary at the embassy and very happy about it. Leaving his home in Arizona for the Foreign Service, he had had the luck to catch London for his first post—a dizzying transition from sleeping on his saddle to wearing white spats and having tea with duchesses. He loved it, and he was ready to give his all to the service and his ambassador, but one man dancing alternately with two girls can last just so long. He suggested a walk in the moonlight, and strolled forth with us, one on each arm.

The light lay soft over the sleeping town of Sonning. We stood on an ancient bridge and listened to the silky Thames whispering through its rushes. Purposely we waited until midnight when the ghost of Dick Whittington is purported to ride over that bridge on its perpetual way to London. The village clock bonged through the stillness, but the ghost did not appear. "Isn't it wonderful," we said, "to be in a place where absolutely nothing ever happens?" We sang a little and strolled on. An hour was never more innocuously spent.

Meanwhile, at the house the game ended, and locking up began.

"The girls aren't in," said Mother, who always managed to be aware of life on several levels at once.

"Of course they are," said Father, handicapped by his unusual powers of concentration. "Go and look."

She went, and returned. No, we were not in.

"They must be," Father said. "Look again."

His tone shut off argument, but on a second search we still had not materialized.

By ill luck, someone had complained to him that very afternoon because Dickson had been seen rocking a punt—a dangerous prank on that weedy river. Father's imagination saw it all. "But long it could not be till that her garments, heavy with their drink, pulled the poor wretch from her melodious lay to muddy death." One or two neighbors were roused from sleep with inquiries. It was nearly time to call the police. The hour had somehow reached one when we sauntered smiling in.

Mother came down the hall to greet us, throwing off sparks. We were used to that and had developed a protective armor against her explosions. Her fire fell harmless, but behind her came Father, extinguishing her as the sun does a candle. She vanished.

He was not really wearing a long black cape which swept behind him, nor was he surrounded by a blazing nimbus. He merely gave that impression. Ignoring the others, he addressed himself to me alone. He did not say much.

"You have been unpardonably rude to your hostess, you have humiliated me, and you have disgraced your country. Go to bed!"

That was all he said.

Next morning, and I later learned that it had taken him all night to calm down, we embraced, with tears in the eyes of both. Sam Dickson left without breakfast and scurried into the far end of the train which we all had to take, but he was not further reprimanded. Nevertheless, it was a full month before Father recovered that equanimity which as a rule made our home life so pleasant.

Unknown to us, and far above our heads, his post was difficult that summer. The world still writhed on the dissecting table.

Lord Curzon, famous for an aloof pomposity, wished to know why, if America were really concerned for the fate of Armenia, she would not accept a mandate for that country when the British withdrew.

"I wish," he said, "that the United States would either come in or stay out. They disclaim responsibility and continue to make disturbing suggestions. I'm afraid all we have done is to make a questionable peace in Europe, and leave Asia at war."

Since this was true, Mr. Davis found it hard to counter, but both he and Washington were deeply annoyed when Curzon blandly assured him that he had "intended" to inform the American ambassador about the Anglo-Persian oil agreement before it became public. "A statement I allow myself to doubt," Davis wrote.

Lord Curzon and Colonel House "differed sharply" as to their recollection of certain conversations in Paris. Three times at the Peace Conference Balfour had refused to hear the Persian delegation; and now the treaty had been made without consulting any of the allies. France raged, and all the more because she had not been equally successful in Syria, where her mandate was bitterly opposed.

The harassed ambassador had a new problem of his own, and one which was never to be solved. He found it increasingly difficult to keep in touch with his own government.

"Not a line from Washington about the Persian matter, and I am still empty handed with the Foreign Office. Sent cable reporting Japanese attitude on consortium, which I presume will reach the same pigeon-hole. I am coming to conclude that a diplomat's duties are confined to wondering about matters as to which he is ignorant, and worrying about questions as to which he is powerless. My Kolchak cable also has worked no signs of life."

Then, like a thunderbolt, and with no warning to England, all of the highly confidential correspondence came out in the American press.

"It is a sequence of Borah's resolution of a week since, calling for all documents on the subject. The Senate has conclusively proven its unfitness to be charged with responsibility for the foreign relations of the United States. . . . If informal correspondence of this character is to be published, it will be impossible to carry on diplomatic interchanges."

The "Kolchak cable" referred to a matter under the jurisdiction of Winston Churchill. He had come to the ambassador asking American arms and supplies for Admiral Kolchak in Siberia, "careful to say that the conversation was unofficial as he recognized that it was not the business of his office to communicate with mine." The British were withdrawing their aid in Russia from everyone except Denikine.

Mr. Davis promised to communicate this message, but held out no encouragement. A month later, he met Churchill at a house party and found him still convinced that Denikine would bring down the Bolsheviks. "Churchill is an incurable optimist as to any enterprise of which he has once approved."

The British themselves took steps to hold Churchill back. Lloyd George, in a speech at a lord mayor's luncheon, baldly announced that no more military aid would be sent to Russia. Instead, negotiations were to be opened with the revolutionaries. Father, looking at Churchill, saw him visibly start and redden; and later heard from another cabinet member that the announcement was made without telling Churchill about it in advance, "for the purpose of stopping his adventures." Few in English public life at that time could be found who approved of Churchill. An old member of parliament, who had sat in the House of Commons for forty years without making a speech, was moved to public utterance: "Mr. Speaker, I can't stand this man any longer."

On October 4 the ambassador received confidential word that President Wilson was "gravely ill." On November 19 the Senate voted not to ratify the treaty, even with the reservations which had been attached to it.

When he heard this, Lloyd George expressed the feelings of most Europeans. "The United States was offered the leadership of the world, and you threw the scepter into the sea."

The vote was a blow to Mr. Davis, and doubled the difficulties of American envoys everywhere. "It seems to me to postpone indefinitely any new order of things," he noted sadly. "I am impressed also with the tremendous loss of prestige which any American plenipotentiary will suffer in any future international gathering. There will be a tendency to write them down as mere messengers, whose views can safely be disregarded." Even through his discouragement, he could see the other side. "One cannot but share the disgust which it is evident has affected the American public with regard to the game of international politics as it is played in Europe."

In the midst of such grave worries, the financial pressure was unremitting. "I have spent over twenty thousand dollars of my own funds this year. When I resign for lack of adequate pay, as I shall, I want to make an example of it for Congressional consumption." As a ray of hope for future ambassadors, he went to see the house in Prince's Gate which J. P. Morgan was offering to the government, and thought that it would be adequate as an embassy. When his excellent private secretary was transferred to Prague, he cried out in dismay, "Who will do my lying for me now?"

Through all the upsets, he went on talking about Anglo-American friendship, "the best hope of peace." "With so many English-speaking people, and all *speaking*, it is not surprising that occasional indiscretions occur." At Manchester, he pleased his hearers by quoting their local hero, John Bright. "I am but one man in this audience, and but one man in this kingdom. But so long as I have a tongue to speak, my voice shall be raised in favor of that policy which leads to generous thoughts and generous words, and generous deeds between the two great nations that speak the English tongue."

He spoke at Sheffield, spoke and froze in Edinburgh, unveiled a statue of Lincoln at Hingham, from which the Lincoln family were supposed to have emigrated, received an honorary degree at Glasgow, where the students carried him on their shoulders and dropped him. This he found amusing, and of the vice chancellor he wrote, "I have met no more charming man."

He spoke at Stratford-on-Avon for Shakespeare's birthday. Delayed by a flat tire, he heard the choir shout "Hallelujah!" as he entered, then someone whispered, "You are next." He spoke for five minutes only. "I felt no desire to emulate the usual oration, and was consciously striving to make what I said remembered by its compactness. The experiment was not without risk." At first he feared that he had disappointed, but the speech was widely reported and later made into a record.

Mr. Davis was acquiring a reputation as a speaker. He and Lord Reading, equally fluent, were so often set up to respond to each other that Lloyd George called them "that famous after-dinner team, Reading and Davis." Occasionally Father had the opportunity of making a serious address on historical subjects, "Treaty Making Power in the United States," "The Unguarded Boundary." (Canadian.) This, and the research for it, he enjoyed.

Not all of so many speeches could be successful. After "a *deadly* evening" at the Lyceum Club, John complained to Nell on the way home, "I think that was the worst speech I ever made."

"It was more than that," said Nell, with a candor born of suffering, "it was the worst speech *anybody* ever made."

In spite of all the ambassador could do, Anglo-American relations struck a new low. AMERICA! WHAT'S YOUR GAME? shouted the tabloid, *John Bull.* "Apparently," Father said, "the American eagle is to join the British lion as an election bugaboo."

He wrote out his analysis of the reasons for the trouble.

1) The fall of the pound, which the British blame on war profiteering. $3.36.

2) The failure to ratify the Treaty.

3) American interference in the Irish situation. A reception to De Valera in New York, Sinn Fein bonds sold there, resolutions passed in the Senate approving Home Rule. What madness!

4) Indiscreet statements by prominent Americans. Admiral Sims, "We would as soon fight England as Germany." General Pershing, "We won the war." The suggestion of Secretary of the Treasury Glass that Europe redress the balance by sending gold to the U.S. Clearly impossible.

5) American callousness to human needs as seen through European eyes; a hundred thousand starving in Austria, fifteen thousand massacred by the Turks in Armenia, etc.

6) Prohibition, which the British fear may be catching, and which gives the cartoonists a wonderful chance to poke fun at Uncle Sam.

7) Underlying all these as the combustible material for which they are the sparks, is a latent trade jealousy, a fear of naval supremacy, and of the rise of the U.S.

The illness of President Wilson complicated every situation, for it was impossible to get through to him, or to secure a decision about anything. Privately, Davis thought that a treaty ratified with reservations would be better than one not ratified at all, but Wilson would not have it so. His illness and his isolation intensified his obstinacy.

"Wilson is too Scotch-Irish to change," said Sir Edward Carson.

"I could not but think of my own father," Father remarked, "for to him there was little difference between compromise and apostasy."

Now that the hero was down, the pack turned on him. "A kind word about Wilson has become a rarity. History will be kinder to him than his contemporaries have been," Father wrote in his diary, but added, "I think Cary Grayson was right in recommending that he resign."

American politicians would not keep quiet about the Irish question, which the British considered a purely internal matter. Will Hays, chairman of the Republican National Committee, told Sir Horace Plunkett that his party would come out for the self-determination of Ireland. "We must have the Irish vote." "A callous avowal of political opportunism," Davis said.

As both sides went on committing murders and outrages in Ireland, the outcry in America increased. T. P. O'Connor expressed the opinion that Home Rule would not come until the English had tried repression until they were tired of it, and the Irish had tried Sinn Feinism until they were disgusted. "It's the Irish nurses you had makes you Americans love Ireland so," O'Connor said. "True in my case," John Davis answered.

The moderate voices in England could not be heard above the din. Earl Grey inquired in the House of Lords, "When has the Empire lost by giving too much?" Sir William Harcourt reminded the House of Commons that "resolute government in Ireland has never produced anything but resolute disorder."

They had no effect. The King himself, whose relations with John Davis had been very cordial since the successful American visit of the Prince of Wales, asked, "How can we raise the white flag when the country is in the grip of a gang of outlaws and murderers?"

An equal rigidity was shown by the Irish lady whom Father

asked at lunch to tell him what the Irish really wanted, and who retorted briskly, "Well, we don't want what we've got!"

On February 14, Mr. Davis, with no previous warning, picked up his morning paper and read that Robert Lansing had resigned as Secretary of State. He reacted with one of his rare losses of serenity. It could not be true. Bert would have told him. He cabled. An answer came. It was true, but the difficulties of the situation had prevented saying anything about it in advance. Long friendly letters explained Lansing's side of it in detail.

The withdrawal of Lansing's support could not have come at a worse moment, for President Wilson had just sent a stiff note disapproving the English-Italian agreement as to Fiume and the Adriatic, and threatening to withdraw the treaty if it went through.

The note came late at night, and the ambassador had to get Lloyd George out of bed to deliver it. They had a spirited conversation.

"This is Wilson himself," the prime minister said. "He is back at work again."

Mr. Davis agreed.

"His threat to withdraw the treaty may be his way of relieving himself from his impasse in the Senate."

"I do not think so," Davis said.

"But he does not realize and never would, our difficulties. We, like the French, are bound by a treaty."

"Wilson is not bound by it. He is not only able to do as he says, but he is capable of carrying out his threat." The ambassador felt it proper to sound this note of warning.

"It would be a mad thing for Wilson to kill his own child in this fashion, and wreck the Democratic party."

Mr. Davis sourly and privately observed that Lloyd George

reacted to every problem in terms of domestic politics. Not surprisingly, the reply which the British concocted next day was as stiff as the note had been. Mr. Davis went to Lord Curzon to hope that it could be moderated.

"Wilson must not be left to enjoy a monopoly of reading high moral lectures to the world," Curzon said.

In the midst of this, Father was "haled off" as he put it, to attend two fashionable weddings, that of the daughter of the Dean of Westminster Abbey, and that of the Hon. Mary Cadogan to the future Duke of Marlborough. We were charmed to have his company for the whole day, immaculate and handsome in top hat and cutaway, greeted on all sides with obvious warmth and affection, responding in his simple manner, which was just the same for a charwoman as for a duchess.

But he would stay only a few minutes at the Cadogan reception. "I can't play all day while England and America go to war with each other." We thought that he was joking.

While he was at dinner that night the final British and French reply was handed to him, and he was relieved to find it "Argumentative throughout, but no final slamming of doors." Something had been accomplished after all. He excused himself, went to the chancery, had the reply coded and on the wire to Washington by one A.M. "Good work," he permitted himself to say.

Still mulling over the troubles of Robert Lansing, Father wrote out his own resignation. He did not send it, but the writing relieved his mind.

By the time we took a short vacation on the Riviera in March, he was ready for it. His throat had given out from too much speaking, his digestion from too much dining. The weather had been what the weather is during a London winter. When one morning the sun came out, I was so startled by the glare that I tried to turn off the electric light, thinking someone had left it burning by mistake.

At Cannes we had ten happy days in the sun, gambled at Monte Carlo, saw the *Bataille des Fleurs,* conspicuously failed to win the five-dollar gold piece which Father hopefully continued to dangle before us if either Katy or I would *ever* learn to play a *decent* game of tennis. He spared himself our exhibitions on the courts after one pained view of them, but took us to see Lenglen in the hope of rousing ambition. It was dead.

His respite could not last. The tormented planet did not orbit into a peaceful summer. The French had seized the Ruhr. The Bolsheviks were conquering the Poles and could take Warsaw whenever they wanted it. Lloyd George laughed off Churchill's warnings about the threat of Russia.

"Barbarian armies fight only for loot," he told the American ambassador. "I'll tell you what you do. If you don't want to shake hands with the Bolsheviks, you let us do it, and then you shake hands with us."

The Bolsheviks, by now a *de facto* government, were trying to press their advantage in Lloyd George's attitude. They sent Krassin as their representative to a conference which hoped to reopen their trade with Europe, but which reached no agreement.

Churchill was not the only prophet of doom. The great Paderewski, in his political phase, visited London and told Father that he expected another generation to see the downfall of European civilization and a new invasion from Asia—Chinese or Hindu.

The British did not believe it. They held India securely, so they thought, although they were of two minds as to how to handle it. Acting in the heavy-handed tradition of the old British raj, General Dyer at Amritsar fired without warning into an unarmed crowd of five thousand natives, killing more than a hundred. The liberal-minded coalition government promptly censured and disciplined him. Then Parliament, placing on their record many things better left unsaid, made haste to censure the government for having done so.

"Tory opinions!" Father said. "An outrage and a shame to the white race!"

While Britain tightened her hold on the oil in Mesopotamia and set up an Arab state, Iraq, to defend it, American interests tried to maintain what they called "the open door."

"You are trying to steal our oil," Sir John Cadman complained to the ambassador.

"I didn't know you had any," was the retort.

It was a time of fraying nerves. To make matters worse, no clear expression of policy on any subject could be obtained from Washington. The tragic condition of President Wilson grew worse, and no messages reached him except those which Mrs. Wilson and his secretary Tumulty thought suitable. Wilson could not hold the helm, he would not relinquish it, and so the ship of state drifted rudderless, or yawed and changed course in a surprising manner.

"Your government is inconsistent," Curzon snapped.

"I do not think any allied government has exhibited that virtue since the war," Mr. Davis answered. He had learned that a short retort was sometimes more respected than a diplomatic evasion.

XVI

On a level far below all these troubles, one small facet of Anglo-American relations improved markedly. The embassy girls had fallen in love with London and with England. We began really to appreciate the British during the railroad strike of our first autumn, when Hyde Park reverberated with army lorries delivering milk, wearing "Baby's Little Lizzie" chalked on their sides. The patient, tired-faced people joked as they queued up; solicitous policemen cleared a path for demonstrators who carried posters blazoned DOWN WITH THE KING! A placard carrier shouted, "We don't need a king, we need a president!" "Who will you have for president?" inquired a bystander. The radical waved his arm at Buckingham Palace around which he was noisily marching. " 'Im, of course."

We began to suspect, and history has proved us right, that the British are at their best in a pinch, that they like themselves most when there is a do on, when they can show their humor, their amazing patience, and their unbreakable fortitude.

Once a week during this winter, so gloomy for the world, so cosy within our walls, Katy and I were drafted for duty when Mother was At Home on Thursday afternoons. Father, with the instinct he had developed for evading traps, used to appear at the last moment and greet the last possible guest, enveloped in an air of having just left the Foreign Office in a flap over Fiume, or Mesopotamia, or Smyrna, or Lithuania, or Galicia. The year did not lack places over which flaps might occur.

Lacking his privileges, we girls were expected to help. We learned how to introduce two people whose names we did not know, by muttering and retreating quickly; we learned how to answer the most inane questions with pleasant smiles and no attempt at wit; learned how to look delighted when a latecomer arrived just as the butler was about to remove the tea.

Most of the American colony attended these afternoons at one time or another, and we learned that their feelings about England followed an observable schedule.

At first they were critical. The cold, the stoves, the kitchen sinks, the flats, the rain, the *language!* The attitude of the English people. The long noses down which they looked. Their standoffishness. The impossibility of getting good American food. The vegetables boiled to death, the puddings fortified with glue, the inexpressible liquid which passed for *coffee.* And, recurrent above all else, THE COLD.

Six months of residence brought a subtle change. The Americans had gone into woolen underwear and no longer tried to go out for dinner without something around their shoulders. They had discovered that colds in the head are not caused by cold rooms—the bacteria are frozen out, poor things. They gave up complaining about the food and called it wholesome. The English people were not so unfriendly as they had at first seemed. In fact, a few were really friendly.

When those who had lived in England for a year or more were ordered home, their wives arrived on Thursday to lament. They could not *bear* to leave. So cosy in London, so peaceful, such a comfortable life. Such willing servants, such a fascinating city to walk about in, such dear friends—only a few, but those like members of the family.

If these exiles in reverse went so far as to speak well of the climate—so temperate, so free from extremes, so healthy—we knew that London had them in its grip. They would go home, but they would come back, come back again and again; and when they did return those few close English friends would greet them as though not a day had passed, nor a mile of water rolled between, and the less intimate acquaintances would say, "You've been away for a while, haven't you?"

By spring, even the junior Davises had passed into the third phase. We too found London comfortable. For our Tuesday tea dances quite a number of girls and even young men turned up. At the winter parties we did not have to recite the alphabet. We had discovered an inexhaustible pool of escorts for emergencies in the younger personnel of the embassy. Would these dedicated souls refuse to go out with the daughter and niece of their chief? No. The number of friendly young Britons increased as well. The transition from cold to warm came suddenly if it came at all. At one dance, as vague and distant as ever, at the next, some mental calculation having been totted up and come out on the credit side, he would repeat the most intimate details of his life, even to his grandmother's last words. The unpredictability of the change gave it a fascination.

It was easy to be entertaining when we needed only to sit silent and let two impossibly handsome young men talk across us about hunting. At last the hunting season ended. We breathed easier and went down to supper at our next dance with anticipation. They talked across us about polo. A horse is a horse is a horse.

At the weekend parties to which we were occasionally invited with the family, we enjoyed the British way of throwing the old and the young together, to the mutual pleasure of both. We heard Father sing Scottish lays with the Geddes brothers and Welsh ballads with Lloyd George. Cromwell came to life for us at Chequers, where his death mask hung beside his own letter describing the battle of Marston Moor, both relics of the days when the house belonged to his daughter. We saw the iron cot on which the Duke of Wellington had died at Walmer Castle. We heard John Drinkwater read his Oliver Cromwell to the guests at Hinchinbrooke. We visited Holkham, where the old Earl of Leicester stubbornly held to the will of his progenitor Edward Coke, which he showed to us.

> If any of my descendants sell any of the property I have left them, I pronounce such person to be ungrateful and unthankful to such an affectionate, loving, and provident ancestor.

Lord Leicester, in his eighties, would not sell one of his ten thousand acres, nor a painting, nor a book. He knew very well that a change was coming. "They can do what they like with it when I am gone." Meanwhile he lived in the old style. A blustery, twinkly old gentleman with a short white beard, he reminded me of the Major, and he ran his household with as firm a hand.

"It's seven thirty, Miss Julia. Breakfast is at eight, and His Lordship likes everyone to be punctual."

The weekends for young people only tended to become what our new friends called "a frightful rag"—beds upset on top of people in the morning, wet sponges under pillows, games of sardines, chicken-foot, or musical chairs. At Warwick Castle the young men put recalcitrant girls into Guy of Warwick's great kettle, which stood by the window in the hall—not to boil them, but to smother them with pillows.

While we were having all this fun, a small cloud was coming up on Father's horizon. Back in the United States friends, and then politicians, and then officials, began talking of him as a possible Presidential candidate.

He considered this nonsense. When the inquiries persisted so that they could not be ignored, he returned to all letters the same reply: "I could not refuse the nomination if it came, for that would be to fly in the face of fate. But on my word I cannot muster either the desire, or the will, or if you please the courage, to invite the blow."

To his English friends he said, "If I am nominated for President it will be under the Selective Service Act."

To avoid any suspicion of seeking the nomination, he decided not to go home on leave until after the convention. This was a personal sacrifice, for the need of arranging his affairs weighed on him more heavily than ever.

"Forty-seven years old," he wrote in his diary on his birthday, "and still in government service, and in a sense my professional career still to begin."

When the Democratic convention was held in June, excited reports said that it looked like McAdoo or Davis. Mr. Asquith, who had known both the rewards and the punishments of popular favor, met Father at a dinner.

"My dear Ambassador, my dearest wish for you is that you do not get it."

"Amen," said Mr. Davis.

When James Cox was nominated on the forty-fourth ballot, he experienced "an intense relief. Now I can and must return to my plans for the future."

I tried to feel with my father's heart about this new disturbance—tried is the wrong word for a reaction so spontaneous—and shared his relief when he was passed by. Also I had at this time more engrossing interests. With May the season opened, the great balls began again, but now how different in aspect!

"I have struggled to give you a good education," Father said, "but it has all gone to your feet."

With Mother's help behind the scenes, he had relaxed his attitude about chaperonage. Even English girls had more freedom during their second season. The only remaining rule was that we must stay together.

"Why should I worry about you?" he inquired. "You go out by daylight, and you come home by daylight."

So there were the embassy girls, having lasted through the evening on ice water, so appallingly full of natural high spirits that they were ready to jump through the drum when the orchestra packed up, although we never carried out the threat. The danger of submerging in the pool around the door had lessened, the blessing of the English system of engaging dances by word of mouth had been discovered. It meant that you never had to dance with anyone you did not fancy.

"I'm so sorry, I'm afraid I'm booked through missing eight—was it missing four I said? I'm frightfully sorry, I thought it was missing three—I waited, and there you were galloping about with Edwina."

We maintained that the same meats in aspic, the same mousses of salmon and chicken were carried by the caterers from ball to ball throughout the season. Certainly the same orchestra pounded away, the same red carpet and awning ran to the curb before each stately door. The same little old man in a top hat and a long coachman's overcoat sprang about every night with a lantern, shouting for the carriages—horseless, of course. He changed his cockade according to the livery of the host, but otherwise he varied not. Always a white-faced London crowd hung about the entrances to watch the glitter. His shouts went forth over their heads.

"The King of Spain . . . The Marquis of Salisbury . . . The Duke of Devonshire . . . Admiral the Earl Beatty . . . Mr. Lloyd George (that would be for Megan) . . . The Prince of Wales . . . The American Ambassador . . . (for us, the ambassador was sleeping peacefully).

Buckingham Palace held its first court since 1914. Such a backlog of aspirants had accumulated that eight hundred and forty were disposed of in an hour and fifteen minutes, passing before the throne, making their two curtsies, backing away, while the King and Queen smiled and nodded like gracious mandarin dolls. To save room trains were forbidden, and with them went feathers. Flashing tiaras and gold-encrusted uniforms made up for it as the whole company sank and rose like wheat in the wind when their majesties entered and walked down the long gallery.

The American ambassador had been limited to presenting only six ladies, which caused him some unpopularity, but he was proud of his winning entries when they appeared.

That spring Mother planned a dinner for the King and Queen which almost turned into disaster when her secretary, given an alternate list from which to fill in after refusals, sent out both lists at once. As a result, too many people were coming who might be expected to sit in the same seat. Another royalty must be provided to prevent a shattering of protocol, and Princess Helena Victoria, by then a good friend, obliged. The Princess Mary, now Countess of Harewood, came without her brothers, to head the table for the younger set. A pink-faced girl with blowy hair, she shared the desperate shyness which plagued her family.

The King, who is the head of every house he visits, of course had to act as host, and took Mother out to dinner. It was a triumph when that early-retiring sailor stayed until after twelve.

"It is very foolish of you people to assassinate your Presidents," he told Father over the cigars. "We (and he meant royalty) could be got rid of once and for all if they were to kill all of us, but so long as one man was left alive he would be a possible President of the United States."

Royalties in Europe that summer often thought and talked of assassination, haunted by the fate of the Tsar and his family. The Queen of Spain talked to Father of the bomb thrown at her carriage on her wedding day, which had spattered her gown with the blood of one of her gentlemen-in-waiting. "My husband says that he is indifferent to death so long as it comes in the dispatch of duty. He has never cared to die but with his boots on. For myself, I could stand being killed, but I have a horror of torture."

British royalties might speak of these dark matters, but they felt no real fear. Through the centuries, following the English system of compromise, of giving a little here and pulling back a little there, they had relinquished oppressive prerogatives gradually and constitutionally. ("Nobody pays any attention to what I say around here," the king once commented to Father in a fit of annoyance.) Their compensation was the genuine devotion of their people. They knew themselves a symbol of unity, a rallying point where conflicting opinions met in patriotism, the "button on the Empire's coat." They were defenders of the new divine right of kings, the right to serve their people. British royalties do not have an easy life, for royal legs may never tire, royal faces never fall, but they are sustained by a sense of dedication to a high duty.

There were so many balls that summer that sometimes we went to four in a single night and walked home through the London dawn bowing elaborately to the milkmen and postmen, who returned our salutes in the same spirit.

The Duchess of Albany, aunt of the King, sponsored a charity ball at Devonshire House just before it was pulled down. It was the first of the great houses to succumb to the wind of change, already felt as a cold breath. The duke had left it. It stood empty, awaiting its execution. Like an aristocrat on the way to the guillotine, it put on a last bright smile for this one night. Now there is not one great house in London still occupied by a private family.

For this last memorable night, Devonshire House returned to its great days. The guests wore costumes of the eighteenth century. Four embassies provided a set of eight each to dance a quadrille. Our right legs stiffened from learning to curtsy in the old-fashioned way with the left elegantly straight on the floor —an athletic exercise far removed from the modern bob. The young military aides who had been drafted for this duty suffered unconscionably, but the eye of their colonel was stern upon them.

"Flirt with me, Ham," I said to my partner as we held our hands high in the air and smiled at each other under them, drawing lightly together and then stepping back for another curtsy and bow.

"Damn it," Ham answered, leering at me from under his white wig in a tortured effort to comply, and arching his lace-ruffled wrist, "I see why men in those days got drunk and rolled under the table rather than join the ladies."

From Ascot to Cowes the season whirled on, apparently as impervious to the storms of the world as a flight of butterflies in the last sunshine before a tornado. The shabby, white-faced Londoners watched us come and go. These were the poor, but not the *very* poor, those housed at a safe distance from the West End. In the middens of Limehouse and Cheapside that summer, some babies were fed on cocoa and water because their parents could not afford milk. We did not know about them, but they knew about us.

The ambassador held his course through one gloomy disturbance after another, but all these troubles were over the heads of the junior members of his family. We had passed into the fourth and incurable stage of love for London. We even liked the climate.

But our time was up. Father could at last plan his trip to America. He would come back to England, he told us, but only long enough to wind up his affairs. He would not bring us back with him for so short a stay. Miss Davis would return to Wellesley to renew that education not entirely devoted to the *feet.* Miss Watson would return to her parents in Indianapolis.

Once Father, ordinarily so easy-going, made a decision, we well knew that argument availed not. At rounds of parties with those now so close English friends, we despaired and "molded" (the current phrase) with an abandon only youth can afford. The S.S. *Olympic* inexorably sailed, and we were on it.

When the orchestra played "Alice Blue Gown," a tune not noticeably sad, but for us packed with associations, we dashed for our cabin—and our last view of England, like our first, was watery, but not because of rain.

XVII

The two months which my father spent on leave in America were notable for two reasons. He joined the New York law firm of Stetson, Jennings, and Russell—soon to be Davis, Polk, Wardwell, Gardiner and Reed—and he was unable to confer with his chief, his President. In fact, he could not see Wilson at all.

Mrs. Wilson invited him to lunch and apologized for the President's "nervous dread of seeing people." "A curious inaccessibility for the leader of a great party and the Chief Magistrate of a nation," Davis wrote.

He worked with the new Secretary of State, Bainbridge Colby, on the note concerning Mesopotamian oil, and was told that Wilson wished him to return to London, but that if he meant to resign in January as he had stated, the President preferred to appoint a successor immediately. Colby privately urged Davis to stay until March, since he did not like the appointee whom Wilson had in mind. Frank Polk, who was the other senior partner in the new law firm, joined in the urging, and Father agreed to finish his term.

"Like a circus horse scenting sawdust," as he put it, he made a few speeches in the going Presidential campaign. At Cooper Union he spoke for the League of Nations. He talked at Clarksburg, then traveled to Cleveland, where he arrived in a heavy rain, was not met, had to call headquarters to find out where the meeting was, discovered that it had been adjourned from a tent on the outskirts of town to a lodge hall, where only two hundred faithful mustered. Before he caught the midnight train for New York, he wired his friend the campaign manager to know "whose skin this should be taken out of," and added in his diary a comment which was to mean more to him later on: "again the folly and selfishness of local campaign committees."

What price an ambassador in American politics? Very little. About this time an old farmer came into Aunt Emma's Red Cross office in Clarksburg and asked:

"Are you the sister of John W. Davis?"

"Yes," she said proudly.

"Well, what happened to him? Did he die?"

The choice of a law firm proved happier than the forays into public life. From among excellent offers, John Davis characteristically selected not the largest firm, not the one which offered the most money or even the greatest share of the profits, but the one which promised the most congenial companionship, the greatest independence, the freest hand.

He spent some time with his sister in Clarksburg and her current convicts, and was pleased at the reception given him by his fellow townsmen. He dropped off the five-fifteen train at Shenandoah Junction and walked across the fields to Media, as he had done so long ago. In November he sailed back to

England, followed by loud wails from Wellesley and Indianapolis.

He arrived at his post in "a London particular," could not see across the street, and recorded that night that he found the old city "foggy, staid, quiet—and as attractive as ever." Obviously the ambassador, like his family, had passed into the fourth and incurable stage of Londonitis.

As representative of an outgoing administration soon to be replaced by a different party, he observed a difference in his status.

"It is hard," said Lloyd George in a confidential talk, "to have no one with whom to do business."

"The outgoing administration can only patch holes in the roof," Davis answered, privately accepting "this clear intimation of my status at present."

To add to his sense of marking time, a note about the Near-Eastern oil was sent directly from Colby to Curzon, by-passing the embassy. The ambassador protested, and was told that "direct communication was intentional, and approved by high authority."

"Which I take to be another evidence that I do not enjoy the maximum of favor with said authority, a fact which causes me no grief. I am not ashamed of the service I have rendered his administration. As for Wilson, such admiration as I have for him as a leader is due solely to his boldness, his devotion to democracy, and his genuine hatred of privilege. For the man himself, I confess that his patent pettiness of soul fills me with the same disgust which has infected all those who have been near him, save the sycophants and time-servers, and which is responsible for the cold hatred that denies him sympathy even in his illness."

This was quite an outburst for my even-tempered father, but he could still be fair-minded, and when Wilson received the

Nobel Peace Prize, he acclaimed it as a well-deserved award. In spite of the troubles which every American in the headless administration was feeling, Father's relations with the British government, and with his many personal friends, had never been more cordial or more confidential.

Lloyd George invited him to a small house party, eagerly accepted, where in long walks together they discussed every problem of the day. The prime minister told him in confidence that he had sent a personal letter to the President in July, dealing with the European situation, which had not only never been answered, but never acknowledged as received. It was "another sidelight on the melancholy state of affairs in Washington," but the visit afforded "two days of most interesting conversation with one of the most vital of living politicians."

Other members of the Cabinet now talked to Davis with a frankness accorded to few, even telling him of their internal disagreements, and the troubles they had with each other—so unavoidably a part of the democratic process.

Winston Churchill came in to ask advice about selling to Hearst the serial rights for the book he was writing about the war. Davis cautioned him against allowing it to be distorted into anti-British propaganda in Hearst publications.

"I told him that I thoroughly disliked and distrusted Hearst, and would advise him to cushion himself by putting his publisher forward to make the contract. Asked him how he had time to do such work. He said he had most of it in his head already and would dictate all narrative portions, writing only introductions and 'purple passages'. Expressed regret at my approaching departure, etc, etc."

Rudyard Kipling expressed the same regret, but added, "I knew Harding was a political genius as soon as he invented that filthy word "normalcy" which is so exactly what people want."

The shy Sir James Barrie darted out to the Davis car as they were leaving a dinner party. Looking away from them he muttered, "I thank you for all the work you have done for the two countries."

"I am sorry I have not done more," Father said.

"You have done magnificently," Barrie answered, and hurried off.

The Davises were the only foreigners invited to Chequers for the weekend when Lord Lee of Fareham transferred that estate to the nation, to be the permanent country home of the prime ministers. Lloyd George accepted it, and his name is first in the great window where all his successors are also inscribed.

"If a radical ministry should come in," Lord Lee said, "it will steady it to be reminded by the surroundings at Chequers of all that went to make up the past of England."

Lloyd George acknowledged this in his acceptance. "I came into politics as an iconoclast, determined to tear down. I realize now that it is equally necessary to construct and to recognize the things that are worth preserving. Party life is one of constant strain, and under the storm of criticism a party officer has the feeling of a hunted animal looking first here and then there to see from what quarter the blow will come, and constantly feeling that he must keep his claws sharp and be ready to use them."

When the final deed of surrender had been witnessed by those present, the Lees drove away to their sister's home. They left behind the historical treasures of the house, the Cromwellian relics collected when it belonged to his daughter, the household equipment, even their own wedding presents. The butler, Filey, who had been with them for twenty-five years, was left like the silver. He came in tears to draw Father's curtains next morning.

"Terrible parting last night, Your Excellency."

"Altogether it was a depressing ceremony," my father wrote. "No one present could, I think, appreciate the spirit which moved them to give up so handsome a home on which so much care as well as money had been spent, and which represented such a large part of their individual fortune; and the form in which it was done gave the impression of making the hair-shirt as rough as possible. There was the uncomfortable sensation one feels on the return to the house of the deceased after the drive to the cemetery. As Riddell put it, it was like witnessing a nun's taking of the veil, where first one garment and ornament and then another is laid aside. The fact that they had even gone so far as to prepare their tomb on the top of Beacon Hill emphasized the funereal suggestion. None the less the gift is a very splendid and generous one, and the idea behind it entirely noble."

When Lord Reading was offered the appointment as Viceroy to India, he consulted with John Davis as to whether to take it. The friendship between the two men had deepened to an instinctive understanding of each other's minds. One night the Davises dined with the Readings, and went next morning to Westminster Abbey to see the earl installed as a Knight of the Bath, England's great honor. He did not appear in the procession.

John pointed out to Nell a passage in the printed oath: "You shall be steadfast in the Faith of Christ." On the way home they called at the Readings to see if he were ill, but John's surmise had been correct. Lord Reading, born Isaacs, a Sephardic Jew who could trace his ancestry for seventy generations, had read the oath the night before, had called the palace to inquire whether he might swear to be "a faithful servant of the Supreme Being," had been told that the oath could not be changed, and had declined the honor.

"His attitude does him credit," wrote Davis, descendant of so many fighters for freedom of belief.

Lord Bryce invited the Davises to lunch, *en famille*. At eighty-two he had just finished his *History of Democracy*, and meant to rest by writing about his travels before he attacked his life of Justinian. He was as usual out of sympathy with the government, thought the British should get out of Mesopotamia, opposed monopoly in oil, saw no objection to America having as large a navy as she wanted to pay for, detested the reprisals in Ireland, and thought a Labor government would be quite capable of letting Ireland become independent and of losing India. "Truly a wonderful man, and younger at eighty-two than many at sixty."

King George and Queen Mary also asked the Davises to lunch alone, and after the meal the queen took Mother to her apartments so that the men might have a confidential talk.

"The King said it had always been his dearest wish, as it had been his father's, to see close co-operation between the two countries, and he had hoped the war might make it permanent —not perhaps an alliance, for that might bring the rest of the world to combine against the Anglo-Saxon bloc; that he saw no reason why the interest of the two countries should conflict anywhere, certainly neither of us wanted more territory, and he thought Great Britain might be taking too great a burden with her mandates, mentioning Palestine, Mesopotamia, and Egypt by name. But—asking my pardon for speaking plainly—there was one point on which British opinion was keenly sensitive, namely supremacy at sea; that the ill-feeling toward Germany began with the Kaiser's effort to build a large navy, about which he was vainer even than about his army; and that if a similar competition sprang up between Great Britain and the U.S. it would breed similar feeling.

"I expressed my agreement that a race in building would ruin both of us, but I added that not only was it easy to excite the vanity of a people by the promise of a larger navy than any other, but that America felt with her outlying possessions and the Canal, that she must be supreme in her own waters and along her coasts.

"He assented. Then, said I, there is Japan, which is arming, not as I believe for aggression against either Great Britain or the United States, but in pursuance of her determination to be supreme in Asia. I expressed the hope that the proposed naval conference between Great Britain and the United States and Japan might be brought about.

"This brought forward the Japanese treaty, as to the renewal of which he said he could not express an opinion, but which was never intended to operate in any contingency against the United States.

"He asked me if I would see Harding on my return, and was plainly anxious that I should convey to him what he had said about the navy.

"On leaving, he and the Queen presented us with their autographed photographs, and bade us good-by in most cordial fashion."

The King's cordiality went beyond official politeness. Years later, talking with another American, he could still say, "It seems a pity that every time you send us a chap we like, such as John Davis, you take him away from us."

Whether the King liked him or not, the administration had changed, and the ambassador had reached the end of his money. The last arrangements were made, the lease terminated, the servants given notice, except for those who stayed on with the new regime. Father sold the Pierce-Arrow which he had bought secondhand from an American general, and smartened up by painting it black instead of khaki. Out of sentiment he kept the eagle which had been a mascot on the hood.

The embassy staff presented the Davises with a silver platter and an engraving; the American newspapermen brought in a case of Dunhill pipes. "A very decent lot. I never had one of them let me down by printing what I said off the record."

Departure day was March 9, with all due speed after the inauguration. Lord Charnwood, who had by then written his life of Lincoln, came with his wife at eight in the morning to say good-by. At the station many gathered, including the Spanish, Italian, Japanese, and Brazilian ambassadors, the Bryces, Midletons, Sandhursts, Readings, Lady Harcourt, even Lord Curzon, and the whole embassy staff, giving three cheers as the train pulled out.

The Admiralty paid a most unusual honor by sending from Southampton a convoy of nine destroyers flying the Stars and Stripes at the peak, lined up in two squadrons of four with a pilot in the middle, to escort the departing ship to the middle of the Channel. Only one other American ambassador had ever been given such an escort—Whitelaw Reid, in his coffin, having died in London.

The retiring ambassador telegraphed his last message.

"Mr. Davis is grateful to the British Admiralty for the courtesy of its convoy. He is glad to have as his last sight of England the representatives of the valiant British Navy, which has done so much to make the seas safe for the commerce of the world."

He made a last notation in his official diary, and with those words closed the book. Nothing more was ever written in it.

"A stop at Cherbourg, out to the open sea, and Home!

"It is the end of a great adventure."

XVIII

London gives up her secrets slowly, but New York pretends to have none. London is brown and smoky sandstone, telling a stranger nothing at first, but warmly livable within. New York is obsidian, and all the hard glitter is not on the surface.

In London acquaintances look one over, but once inspection has been passed, friendship is steady. In New York, strangers are greeted with glad cries of cordiality—"we *must* get together"—and rapidly forgotten on parting. It is not that New Yorkers are hardhearted, it is that there is so much they can do, and they wish to do it all. In a city where light, space, and above all privacy, are luxuries beyond the reach of most, a glancing approach may be the best protection. At least it is the one used.

We arrived in the midst of Prohibition, the era of unbeautiful nonsense. The city glittered and quite literally careened. For the first time in my existence, I felt an alien. The basic values of the English gentry had not been too different from those of my childhood. In New York I could not find out what the values were. The people seemed like paper dolls, all front and no back. The key word seemed to be *more*: more fun, more excitement, more money, more drink, more friends, or rather acquaintances, for there is of necessity a limit to the number of friends a heart can hold. It took me some years to find them in Manhattan.

With the years in London ended the longest time I ever spent or was to spend under my father's roof. I went back to Wellesley, where life proved like a pair of shoes grown too tight. I came down to live in New York and go to Barnard, where by resolutely taking no course which did not come on Monday, Wednesday, or Friday, I managed a good deal of time to myself.

Financial stringency, which had really caught up with the Davises at last, precluded any entertaining for me. I was sent forth, cold, to New York parties. It said ten on the cards, and Mother, still diplomatically punctual, saw that I arrived at ten, to sit in an empty drawing room and watch the butler light the fire and beat up the cushions, or to wait in the ladies room at the Ritz or the Plaza until a chattering group of girls who had gone to school together came in from some dinner party. Lack of social ambition kept me from taking this too seriously, but I felt lost.

All four of my grandparents had died, the last, Grandmother McDonald, just as Father left London. "The most saintly woman I have ever known is no more," he said. Aunt Emma lived alone in the echoing house in Clarksburg; Anne, Marshall, and Will carried on at Media. The homes of my childhood had shrunken, had altered. I needed to get away from them for a time in order to find them again.

As soon as the college year ended, I escaped, to spend the summer with a friend in London, and then to visit the Viceroy in India with the Erleighs, Lord Reading's son and daughter-in-law.

Even the redoubtable Mrs. Davis, our steering committee in practical matters, found New York difficult. It took her some years to achieve anything like comfortable living there. She tried an apartment on the second floor near Grand Central, where the noise kept us from hearing voices in our rooms when we opened our windows at night. Fleeing from this, she tried a house on Ninety-first street with a Queen Anne drawing room and Mary Anne bedrooms. Everything had to be rented furnished, since the money for furniture had not yet come in.

Beyond the housing problem, Mother was facing an upheaval within herself. For the first time in her married life, her husband was embarking on a career in which she could be no real help to him. He was busier than ever, but at work which took him away from her, work which she could not share. She could and did continue to see that he was comfortable, but she was not content. She felt herself growing older, she saw herself less beautiful, and she fought the inevitable with passion.

During this period of readjustment, Father was more fortunate than the women of his family. With relief, with joy, and with absorption, he had gone back to practicing law. At first he suffered from his usual self-doubt. Could he hold his own as a lawyer in the competition of a big city? It turned out that he could.

In the beginning he worked harder than his youngest clerk. A client asked him a question about New York law to which he had "not a glimmer of an answer." This searing experience threw him into such a cold sweat that he determined it should never happen again. He had to wait six months before he could claim residence and be admitted to the New York bar. By the time this occurred he had mastered the statutes of the state.

He had not only his work, he had partners, who proved congenial, soon to be loved like brothers. His range expanded. The law was, as it had always been, not only his occupation, but his amusement, his hobby, his life. "I never had any ambition," he said, "except to be a pretty good lawyer."

He relieved his feelings about the underpayment of foreign envoys by testifying before the House Foreign Affairs Committee on the Rogers bill for reorganizing the diplomatic and consular service.

"I am quite sure that my establishment in London was more

modest than that of any other ambassador there. . . . Living without any ostentation it cost me roughly three times my salary every year. . . . When a man goes abroad as a representative of the United States, he is charged on the theory that he represents the richest country on earth. You cannot get away from that situation."

Now that he was working for himself at last, he began to feel sure that he could make a living. He purchased an ugly but comfortable house at Locust Valley, near friends, comparatively cheap, and furnished, still an important consideration. That the furniture was as ugly as the house did not matter. "Only the chimneys are sticking out above the mortgage," he said. He named it Mattapan, from an Indian word meaning "I sit down," and sit down he did for the rest of his life. Across the road a friend with either too much or too little sense of humor named his estate Dunrobin.

I was married from Mattapan in the first autumn of Father's ownership. The winter before, I had been invited to stay on with the Readings, go on the annual tour of native Maharajahs, visit Calcutta for the races. Reports—exaggerated—had made Father fear that I might marry out there, and he sent for me to come home. It did him no good. Within a few months I became engaged and went to live for three years in Copenhagen. But he had suffered too much himself from parental opposition ever to stand firmly against anything I wished, either then or later.

Mattapan suited him. On the top floor he had his study, a big room with a distant view of Long Island Sound over a sweep of lawn, most of which belonged to a neighbor. ("What river is that?" asked the wife of Colonel House.) In this retreat were his law books, and here he could shut himself up "in the monastic seclusion of my briefs." So long as he had this eyrie, Mother could do as she liked with the rest of the house. Sometimes he failed to notice an improvement for weeks after it had happened.

"Johnnie, you are so spoiled," she said. She took up gardening as an avocation.

He welcomed dark Sunday mornings. "Thank God it is raining and I don't have to play golf." The *Times* quickly skimmed, he would disappear upstairs and that would be the end of him until the current dog, Jock, then Piper, then McGuiness, was sent with a folded note announcing a meal.

Golf he played only for the companionship in it. He liked to go swimming when he came home from the office on hot nights, but never learned anything except the backstroke, churning the water for a few seconds and stopping refreshed. He still rode occasionally, but Mother would not permit him to keep a horse on the place. Bridge he enjoyed, stoutly defending what he called the Davis Intuitional System to partners often astonished and sometimes aggrieved. His real diversion was his work.

Life seemed at last to settle to a comfortable pace, a steady rack which could go on for miles. Then another surprise attack developed.

The lightning which had spared him in 1920 struck in 1924. He was nominated as the Democratic candidate for the Presidency.

The storm had rumbled for some time. Clarksburg organized a Davis-for-President club, and the idea spread through West Virginia. Early in 1924 an admirer wrote urging him to free himself of "the Wall Street taint," by getting rid of such an unpopular client as J. P. Morgan. At first Father answered this facetiously.

Dear Mr. Huntley:

I have your note of the 12th and thank you for the interest which inspires it. I have never been much of a success at the drama, as perhaps you know. After all, "the cool sequestered vale of life" is not without its advantages. As for Wall Street, was it not Mark Twain who said that all money had a double taint—'taint yours, 'taint mine?

Yours with regards,
John W. Davis.

Mr. Huntley found this reply "irritatingly goodhumored"; wrote twice more, and at last received a serious answer.

If I were in the market for the goods you offer, I would not complain of the character of the consignment, although I notice that you do not guarantee delivery. The price you put on them, however, is entirely too high.

I am to abandon forthwith a law practice which is both pleasant and within modest bounds profitable; to desert a group of professional colleagues who are able, upright, and loyal. If this were all, I would think your figures pretty stiff, but you are really asking something more.

I have been at the Bar nearly thirty years, and with the exception of ten years spent in public life, I have enjoyed during the whole of that time a practice of an extremely varied character.

At no time have I confined my services to a single client, and in consequence I have been called upon to serve a great many different kinds of men; some of them good, some indifferently good, and others over whose character we will drop the veil of charity. Indeed, some of my clients—thanks perhaps to their failure to secure a better lawyer, have become the involuntary guests for fixed terms of the nation or the state. Since the law, however, is a profession and not a trade, I conceive it to be the duty of the lawyer, just as it is the duty of the priest or the surgeon, to serve those who call on him.

No one in all this list of clients has ever controlled or even fancied that he could control my personal or my political conscience. I am vain enough to think that no one ever will. The only limitation upon a right thinking lawyer's independence is the duty which he owes to his clients, once selected, to serve them without the slightest thought of the effect which such a service may have upon his own personal popularity or political fortunes. Any lawyer who surrenders this independence, or shades his duty by trimming his professional course to fit the gusts of popular opinion, in my judgment not only dishonors himself, but disparages and degrades the great profession to which he should be proud to belong. You must not think me either indifferent or unappreciative if I tell you in candour that I would not pay this price for any honor in the gift of man. . . .

What is life worth, after all, if one has no philosophy of his own to live it by? If one surrenders this to win an office, what will he live by after the office is won? Tell me that!

Believe me, cordially yours,
John W. Davis.

That, John thought, should close the subject, but after two weeks of rumination, Mr. Huntley asked permission to print the letter. Protesting that "to print is hell," Father agreed, so long as enough could be printed to show his entire meaning. "The sentiments therein expressed are not subject to change."

The letter was reprinted all over the country, and drew much editorial comment, most of it favorable. John W. Davis went on practicing law.

When the Democratic Convention met in New York, the Davis-for-President-Home-Town-Club took a room at the Waldorf and put pictures of their favorite son in the corridors.

"You are making me ridiculous," their candidate said.

"John, you are not responsible for what your fool friends may do," Clem Shaver answered.

The matter might have ended there, but for the worst deadlock in political history. William G. McAdoo and Alfred E. Smith both lacked the two-thirds majority, both had about the same number of votes, neither would release their delegates. Delegates pledged to outsiders hung on stubbornly for fear of climbing on the wrong bandwagon. West Virginia stood for her favorite son, and Alabama cast twenty-four votes for

Oscar Underwood so often that the phrase passed into the slang of the day. This went on for one hundred and two ballots.

John W. Davis tried to ride out the convention from the detachment of Long Island, but as excitement mounted he and Nell came in to stay with the Frank Polks. Yelling, perspiring, exhausted, and obstinate, the convention struggled on.

While the one hundred and third ballot was being cast, Father sat in the Polk library, reading a book. Mrs. Polk, glued to the radio, called to him, "John, you've got it!"

For a man of his temperament it was like being sucked into a maelstrom. He had his full share of both pride and ambition, but none of the joy in projecting himself to the public which marks the successful actor or politician. That night, behind his closed bedroom door, he went into the worst panic of his life. He swore that the job was too big for him and he could not go on with it. He held Nell's hands and begged her to stand by him —as if there were a possibility of her doing anything else. The panic passed with the darkness. By morning he had settled into the collar like the draft horse he called himself, and began to plan the acceptance speech, which he would give in Clarksburg.

Nevertheless, although no one saw him afraid again, the campaign was to him a process of being picked and pulled to pieces by millions of hands, and fed into millions of maws.

When I came home from Copenhagen for the last months of the ordeal, I found the candidate tired. On his rare intervals at home, the house was awash with advisers, politicians, photographers, reporters, and plain ax-grinders. Everyone whittled a chip off the candidate.

He had resigned himself to the invasion of his private life, although he failed to see why the public should care to have him pictured playing with the gardener's little daughter, fond of her though he was. He carried his right arm in a sling because a steel worker had wrenched it from the shoulder socket by grabbing his hand and refusing to let go as the line surged past. He had spoken in halls, armories, tents, and open lots, usually without benefit of a microphone, and often six times a day. He was in the thick of as good a fight as he could make. He had few illusions as to the outcome.

The cleavage in the Democratic party had not healed. Al Smith offered support, but his followers were dragging their heels. Will Rogers summed up McAdoo: "McAdoo went into the hospital and told the doctors to cut something out, and if he got well too soon to put it back and cut it out again." The candidacy of the radical Senator La Follette took more votes from the liberal Democrats than it did from the conservative Republicans. And President Coolidge never moved out from behind the dignity of his office to answer any arguments or meet any attacks. He made only one speech during the campaign, and that to the United States Chamber of Commerce: "This is a business country, and should have a business government."

His opponent tried to get him to express an opinion. "There are gentlemen in this country who believe that the greatest duty a public servant can perform is to keep cool! If scandals break out in the government, the way to treat them is—silence. If petted industries make extortionate profits under an extortionate tariff, the answer is—silence. If the League of Nations or any foreign powers invite us to a conference on questions of world-wide importance, the answer is—silence! The Republican campaign is a vast, pervading, and mysterious silence, broken only by Dawes warning the American people that under every bedstead lurks a Bolshevik ready to destroy them."

Davis could shout as much as he liked. Coolidge publicly expressed the opinion that America was a great nation, and that children should honor their parents.

Father would have thought that he was imposing a fraud on

the public if he had had his speeches ghosted for him, although naturally he availed himself of experts and advisers. When I went through the voluminous campaign papers which came to rest in his attic and were never looked at again until after his death, I found a file of material which he had digested on each issue of the day before he spoke on the subject.

He had kept also the bad press notices, from the editorial which called him "an ineffectual angel beating his wings in the void," to the headlined cover of the *Nation* "Why John W. Davis is not fit to be President." Among the unsorted papers lay a pamphlet on "The Art of Public Speaking." After all his success as a speaker in England, Father was still trying to improve himself—but then he was never a man who thought he had no more to learn.

He was saved from extinction in the hurly-burly by his sense of humor, and cherished the amusing things which happened on his tours, from the old lady at Washington and Lee who cried with tear-filled eyes, "Oh, John, you are awfully proud of me!" to the henchwoman in Jersey City, who had doubts about him until she met him, but then declared, "Sure he's a fine man entirely, and he can park his shoes under my bed any night!"

Some encounters were not humorous. In the Middle West a man came to his hotel room with a letter from the Grand Imperial Wizard of the Ku Klux Klan, then in infamous revival.

"Can I see you alone, Mr. Davis?"

"I have no secrets from Carl Vance. He will stay with us."

The letter offered to deliver certain states to the Democrats if the candidate would refrain from mentioning the Klan during his campaign. It did not ask for active support, only for silence.

Father read it through. "Is that all you have to say to me?" It was. "Then you may say there is no answer." He showed the letter to Carl Vance, then tore it in two.

At St. Louis, in his next speech, he denounced the Klan. In the America to which he was dedicated, no one should be terrorized because of race or religion. To preserve this right he would make any sacrifice and he would not temporize.

He lost all the states which the Klan had promised, many of them southern. He received from the Negroes of St. Louis a silver-plated cup three feet high, thanking him for his services to their race.

When I came home he gave me the same instruction he had given his wife and his sisters. I was to make no speeches. I might, if asked, travel about and attend receptions, trying to be agreeable, but saying no more than politeness required. He was taking no chances on having to explain indiscretions, but more than that, he had the old-fashioned notion that the people should select a man for himself, not for his family. He made no room for us on his special train.

He did, however, take me with him to hear one of his few talks on the radio, then just coming into political use. He had in his pocket a prepared address, carefully timed for the allotted twenty minutes. Babe Ruth introduced him, in one of those strange partnerships that politics makes, and then swung on the microphone talking about the games he had played, until he left the candidate just five minutes' time.

With my modest role firmly impressed upon me, I was haled off by the faithful on several painful tours. A dowager in Washington asked me to speak at a gathering in her house. I replied that I could not speak, but would be glad to attend. When I arrived she seized and kissed me, told me that my grandfather had nearly married her—a flight of fancy—caught my hand and led me through a door. I found myself on a platform in a ballroom, facing two hundred expectant people on gold chairs. Still grasping my wrist so that I could not disentangle it without looking like a woman wrestler, she rushed me to the footlights, let go, and waved both arms in the air.

"Everybody stand up! This is the daughter of John W. Davis, who has come all the way across the sea to make you a little speech!"

With that she left me, while the captive audience could do nothing but rise and applaud.

I longed for the head of Medusa to turn her and them to stone. Mentally I consigned her to the lowest of the seven hells, but had no time to tell her so. I thanked the audience for their reception, which I took as intended for my father; I left the speaking in the family to those better equipped to do it. I sat down. Fortunately there were others on the platform straining for their chance, and the meeting continued.

Affable enough in private life, but shy in public, I found the campaign trying, although no other experience equaled that one in horror. Wherever I went, one attitude repeated itself. The campaign workers expressed the suitable confidence as to the outcome, but when asked how they were doing in that particular district, their faces fell.

"To tell the truth, we are not too sure of it here. But," brightening, "in the next state (or the next county, or the next town, or even the next ward) things are going fine."

Enjoyable or not, these tours were an unforgettable worm's-eye view of the pyramid of American politics, with its broad base of thousands of little workers on whom the prominent politicians rest; its jostling for position on every step of the long climb to the top; and its willingness to put local interests ahead of national ones in order to please the local voters.

"Politics is the science of applied selfishness," Father used to say, and I could see where he got the idea. Then he would add, smiling, "It is the first duty of a politician to get elected."

Election morning found us on Long Island, and the house

quiet at last, since everything had been done that could be done. My husband had come over to join us for the kill, but since he was at that time a nonresident American, we could not vote. Even West Virginia would not have me. I felt the deprivation keenly. To have cast a first vote for my father would have been a satisfaction.

When we came down for breakfast, Father was already at the small table in the alcove, and looked up cheerfully from his egg as if it were a day like any other.

"I am never sure," he remarked, "whether I like best the view over the Sound, or that lovely moving wall of green trees on the other side."

I could not leave it at that. "How are you this morning?"

"Very well, thank you. But not buoyed up with hope."

When they had voted, we went to the Polks' in New York to listen to the returns. Father played bridge all evening. In view of his calm urbanity, no one could appear less calm than he, although the enormity of the disaster was soon apparent. Until then no Democrat had ever been beaten so badly, although Al Smith topped the record four years later. Only when he learned that West Virginia, and even Harrison County had gone against him, did Father show distress. That news gave him a pain which he could not conceal.

As the evening wore on, some of the rest were not so controlled. Harold Hathaway, a young lawyer from Davis Polk, who had been Father's secretary during the campaign, and who had for him the deep affection which he inspired in most young men who worked for him, wandered from room to room with tears rolling down his cheeks. I saved my tears until I went to bed, but I think that Harold and I were crying about the same thing—not the loss of the office, but the pain of seeing John W. Davis hurt. He himself had no tears to shed, either then or later.

It was his first major failure, and no man with his rage for achievement and perfection could be expected to like it. "The whip of scorpions," which as a young man he had feared, was this time well applied. He had not sought the Presidency, he had dreaded its crushing responsibilities; but no American could be indifferent to the possibility of getting it.

He also felt keenly the assumption that he was not a liberal. As a lawyer in Clarksburg he had defended the right to strike for the miners and the glass-workers; in Congress he had helped to draft the Clayton antitrust act, and had personally written its most liberal labor planks; as Solicitor General he had defended the eight-hour law, the Sherman antitrust law, and had overthrown the grandfather clause, which kept Negroes from voting in Oklahoma. He had exhausted his private funds in public service. For only three years of his life had he been "a Wall Street lawyer," and yet the liberals had turned against him.

After the quarrels of the convention it was not likely that any Democrat could have been elected. The party had needed a sacrificial goat to send into the wilderness, and they had found their man. This Father realized, but the magnitude of the defeat cut deeply.

He was, however, philosophically a stoic. Fortune must be accepted with a certain courtesy and outfaced, whether it be good or ill. A man should neither boast of her favors, nor complain of her scorn. Like his favorite, Epictetus, he counted it the mark of manhood that while he could not alter Fortune, Fortune could not alter him.

When everything was over, he and Mother took a short vacation. They stopped briefly in England, where he was asked, "What is the real difference between the Democrats and the Republicans?"

"About six million votes," he said.

There have been defeated Presidential candidates whose

after lives have been spent in bitterness, or in a vain striving for what they had lost. John W. Davis put the experience behind him once and for all. When he had rested, he went back to practice law.

XIX

Since the one ambition of John W. Davis was to be "a pretty good lawyer," as a pretty good lawyer let him be remembered. For the next thirty years the stream of my father's life, so often deflected by unexpected islands, even by sandbars and snags, ran broad and deep in its natural channel. With energy, with application, with relish, he practiced law, and the law gave him a pleasant life. Tall, of good carriage, with the white hair which I never remember as dark, keen, clear blue eyes like his mother's, and a pink face sometimes smiling, sometimes thoughtful, but always serene, he sailed into his later years as gracefully as a ship comes into harbor.

It has been said that he had an unsatisfied yearning for a seat on the Supreme Court. This is not true. The honor was twice offered him, and twice refused. The first occasion came too soon after his return from London, when personal resources were nil. By the time he received the second offer, he was convinced, if indeed he had ever doubted, that his talents and his tastes were for the bar and not the bench. When he was offered the presidency of a great university he was tempted, because of his joy in training young men, and his belief in the importance of the teacher; but love of the law prevailed.

Not only had he attained a mastery of his profession, he believed it a noble calling. He saw the lawyer as a man dedicated to justice, to government under law as the only safe form of government; and he saw the law itself, ever evolving out of the needs of humanity, as the cement which holds society together.

He would amaze and sometimes daunt his partners by taking unpopular cases without pay. He defended Isador Kresel, attorney for the National City Bank, who was disbarred after the downfall of his client. The idea of guilt by such association struck at John Davis's conception of the lawyer's role: not his to judge the client, but to present the case, and let the bench hand down the verdict. In the face of great criticism, and for months on end, he fought for Kresel, and when Kresel was acquitted and restored to practice, he declined a fee.

He defended conscientious objectors without charge; he defended Clarendon County, South Carolina, without charge, he had agreed to take the case of Robert Oppenheimer if it came to court.

It is significant that he wrote a pamphlet on the defenders of Louis XVI, lawyers who risked and lost position, estate, and even life itself, to do a lawyer's duty.

Although the theory was becoming unpopular, he believed that the rich were as much entitled to justice as the poor. In this belief he acted as attorney for J. P. Morgan and Co., when they were under senatorial investigation.

"I lined up the partners and held school every day." Daily behind the scenes he took the role of the investigators, asking embarrassing questions in disagreeable tones, schooling his class in the proper answers, and still more in the proper attitude: never to be caught off guard, never to try to be clever, never to show irritation or take a haughty tone with the representatives of the Senate. Well schooled, Mr. Morgan himself could smile when a publicity-seeking midget jumped into his lap. The firm came well through an ordeal which had seemed to them unthinkable and insupportable. After it was over, the partners wrote a joint letter:

Dear John Davis:

. . . Without your wisdom and sympathetic interest we should have been at a loss how to prepare for the examination before the Senate Committee; without your great legal ability we should not have known how, or to what extent it was wise, to defend our rights . . .

In the course of his practice, he argued more cases before the Supreme Court than any other lawyer had ever done. Although most of his later work was in corporate law and heard in appellate courts, he occasionally gave himself the pleasure of arguing before a jury. "I took out the old fiddle to see if it would play."

His decalogue on the art of advocacy, included in an address to the Bar Association, has been called a Bible for young lawyers.

1) *Know your record from cover to cover.*
(You have now reached a point where you can no longer hope to supply the want of preparation by lucky accidents.)

2) *Change places in your imagination with the court.*
(Try to tell your story as that particular judge would have it told.)

3) *State the nature of your case and briefly its prior history.*
(Judges, like other men, judge each other as well as the law.)

4) *State the facts.*

5) *State next the applicable rules of law on which you rely.*

6) *Go for the jugular vein.*
(There is in every case a cardinal point around which lesser points revolve like planets around the sun.)

7) *Rejoice when the court asks questions.*
(It gives you the assurance that they are not comatose and that you have awakened at least a vestigial interest.)

8) *Read your argument sparingly and only from necessity.*
(A sheet of paper interposed between speaker and listener walls off the mind of the latter as if it were boiler plate.)

9) *Avoid personalities.*
(Sheer futility as a method of argument.)

10) SIT DOWN.
(The fact that you have been allotted an hour more or less does not constitute a contract with the court to listen for that length of time.)

Father's long and successful record of legal activity is open for all to read, but there are public figures who, like some actors, look smaller off stage. With him the opposite was true. The nearer one came to him, the larger he appeared, and those who knew him best loved him most. As his firm grew, he spoke with shame of not recognizing all the young men by sight, but those who had occasion to work with him knew that he was neither disinterested nor aloof. They honored him as a father, and mourned for him like sons.

A vital member of his household for thirty years was Hanson, his butler and general assistant, "who looks after me as if I were his four-year-old daughter." Hanson told him when to buy a new suit or new pair of shoes. Hanson took his old hats and hid them. Hanson, who could make a production out of bringing a glass of water, trailed him with the medicines which the patient had no intention of taking unless he were caught. On a snowy morning, Hanson would stand by the door with the overcoat, the hat, the briefcase, the cigar. At the last moment he would produce the overshoes which he had been hiding behind him. "I think you had better put these on, sir." Fairly trapped, Father would groan and obey. Hanson once wrote him: "They say no man is a hero to his valet, but I can give the lie to that."

One secret of Father's charm was that he had no pose, no public face which he put off and on. When he said in the courtroom that he was a country lawyer trying to get along, he expected a chuckle and heard it, but when the Bar of Clarksburg put a bust of him in the courthouse there, he wrote them in all sincerity that their recognition meant more to him than any honor he had received.

"Who was that, John?" he was asked when he stopped an old hod carrier on a Clarksburg street.

"I don't know. I just felt like talking to him."

The college mates, the early friends, grew fonder by the years rather than estranged. John Davis remained as integrated with his past as with his present.

At least a score of children with whose parents he had some tie of kinship or friendship felt themselves the objects of his particular interest and rewarded him by the eagerness with which they sought his company. With them, and with other friends, he liked to correspond in verse, sometimes amusingly, sometimes reflectively:

I do not sorrow that the Day is spent,
Its toil complete.
The hours that went
So speedily were all with care replete
And each but lent
To toil its burden and to pain its increment.

Yet of them all not one would I subtract
From memory's store,
No thought, no act
Would it not grieve me sorely to restore
For all they lacked,

Since all I am is but of these compact.
"I am a part of all that I have met,"
Odysseus cried,
His sails all set.
So when I move out on the ebbing tide,
May Nature's debt
Be paid without rebellion and without regret.

The lengthening years brought their inevitable sorrows. Mother's health grew increasingly fragile. "It is hard to see her slipping away from me," he said. If she spoiled him by relieving him of domestic worries, he did his share of spoiling also. "It is a real test of my affection," he secretly admitted, "that I have for so long submitted to okra soup and the string bean."

When he reached the stage of being able financially to do as he liked, what he liked was to give pleasure. "The winter in South Carolina will be good for your mother." "Nell wants to go to Greece." "Nell wants to make a garden, so I have bought the adjoining lot." "Is that what you really would prefer to do, Julia? I have discovered in life that the only way you can help people is to help them do as they please."

His only selfish indulgence was salmon fishing, two weeks a year on a river in Canada. The trip diverted him for a month beforehand, as he mulled over his tackle and practiced casting on the lawn—once catching his lower lip. A picture of the river hung over his desk all year, so that he could dream himself into it. "That lovely stream! That peace and quiet!" His face beamed when he mentioned it. On the river he found the simplicity of living which was congenial to him and which his daily life did not afford. If he caught salmon, all but one were sent to friends with verses attached. If he caught none, the trip was not a failure; he sought refreshment of spirit rather than sport.

Improved circumstances made it possible for him to take

care of many people: a trust fund for Em; another for an invalid great-niece; loans to help nephews finish their education, not to be paid back on condition that they some day would do the same for another young man; unrecorded assistance to untold people. "I've never kept track of what I've given away, but I expect it is as much as I've kept."

He paid little attention to his own business affairs. It was not so much a willful neglect, as a matter of not having them on his mind, and forgetting first the things which seemed to him the least important. In the crass twenties he maintained a refreshing indifference to the materialistic trend and had not the faintest wish to compete with his rich neighbors on the North Shore. Since for some time all his income was earned, it was soon clear that the income tax would prevent his amassing a fortune. He worked most of his time for a government which spent the money in ways he could not approve. He grumbled, but not so much as his father would have done.

"Those people downtown, with their feet on the thermometer, worry all the time. When I buy a stock I ride it up and ride it down, and never look at it again. I am convinced that anybody can get rich if he cares more for money than he does for anything else."

In the earliest days of prosperity, he gave me my first piece of real jewelry, a small diamond pin. I lost it in the subway and came home in tears.

"Never mind," he said. "It doesn't matter. Learn not to attach too much importance to material things." There was no suggestion that he might get me another.

When his house was struck by lightning for the third and most serious time, Father was eating dinner alone, solacing himself with a book. Mother was ill in bed upstairs, a nurse in attendance. He heard a deafening thunderclap, but with his usual lack of concern for what did not concern him, he continued to read. Hanson came in with a brisker step than his habitual stately tread.

"I'm sorry to disturb you, sir, but I am afraid that the house is on fire."

"Surely not," said Mr. Davis, not too pleased at the interruption, and went on with his book.

Hanson exited rapidly, re-entered more rapidly still, to announce that the flames were spreading, the fire department had been called, and Mrs. Davis had been brought down to the kitchen in a wheel chair for fear the house would have to be evacuated.

At last moved to investigate, Mr. Davis found the top floor burning brightly. Mother was taken to a neighbor's, and Father came back to see what he could do.

Tons of water, poured in by the fire department, cascaded down the front stairs. Tons of water poured from the sky. Servants and friends scurried about, carrying what they could to the front lawn. Father got his fishing rod first, then began on his books, an armful at a time. On each return to the front hall, by then an inland sea, Mr. Davis, a man whose habits Fortune could not alter, paused to wipe his feet carefully on the doormat.

Although he began to rebuild at once, Mother did not live to see the house restored. They rented next door for six months, and she died there. Among his papers Father preserved two notes from her, each written on the occasion of having to go to a hospital.

Dear Lover,

Tonight I can tell you only this. My years with you have brought me nothing but happiness. You have been the noblest man and the most perfect husband any woman ever had.

Your adoring Nell.

Between the years 1943 and 1945 many sorrows came to Father, for he lost not only his wife, but his sister Emma, and his partner Frank Polk, whom he loved as a brother. In his home nothing could replace the singlehearted devotion which had enwrapped him, the cheerful call which always answered his whistle when he came in the door, the unfailingly ready companionship. The hours of silence gathered.

He did not complain. "I always read the obituaries first in the paper, to see if I am still alive." As the attrition of the years took one good comrade after another, we quoted the words of Stonewall Jackson, driving his men on their incredible marches up and down the Valley Pike.

"Press on, men. Press on. Close up, men. Close up."

With Hanson to assist me, I tried to make everything domestic go as comfortably as usual, outwardly unchanged. The companionship which we missed in my youth was fully ours before the end. I like to think this may have been some compensation.

When Father was seventy-seven, I went with him to England, where Oxford gave him an honorary degree. He had not visited there since World War II, and he grieved over the ravaged city of London as he might have over scars on the face of an old friend. The unforgetting British gave him a royal welcome. We went to Oxford in, of course, a pouring rain. Elegant in a borrowed gown of stiff red silk and an Erasmus-like velvet hat, he took his place at the end of the academic procession as a new honoree should. Two old gentlemen in front of him became so absorbed in their conversation that they stopped to talk, huddled under one umbrella. Those in advance trooped in. The doors of the Sheldonian Theater solemnly closed. Finally someone missed Mr. Davis, who, never liking to thrust himself forward, had forborn to interrupt the conversation of his predecessors. The doors were reopened and he came in, looking as abashed as a boy late for school.

Lord Halifax made the awards in Latin, which Father could read but could not speak. Only two words reached him clearly, and I saw him start. "Calvinus Coolidge."

In his seventy-ninth and eightieth years, he argued two of his most important cases before the Supreme Court. He successfully defended the United States Steel Company from seizure by the government and he failed to save South Carolina from the threat of integration.

His partners urged him not to take the integration case, and I added my voice, but could not influence him. He considered that the law was on his side, and that the case represented a last chance to fight for the individual state against encroaching Federal government. More important still, he believed that for the Negroes themselves the change would come too soon; that the effort to force the issue would rouse antagonisms which time was healing and would cause a bitterness damaging to both Negro and white. He was in favor of starting integration at a college level and letting it work down by a gradual evolution. "If this law goes through, it will set race relations back fifty years."

On the day of the argument I sat in the courtroom next to Mrs. Thurgood Marshall, whose husband, stating at the outset that he did not intend to argue fine points of law, made an impassioned and moving plea for human rights. When he had finished, I congratulated her.

"So you are the daughter of Judge Davis! My husband admires him so much. He thinks he is the greatest lawyer in the country, and every time he has a case down here if Thurgood can spare the time he comes over to listen to him."

The important cases took a toll at times alarming. Father's mind retained its clarity, but his legs disgusted him by turning unreliable. "All that I have ever asked of my body is that it should keep out of my way and let me do my work."

I did not live with him in New York, but I walked up every morning and joined him as he ate breakfast by a window overlooking the park.

Sometimes what I saw did not please me. "Why are you sitting there like a wet eagle?" I had to ask.

"I'm tired of putting shingles on the old roof," he stoutly answered.

When he got to work, his brow cleared, his spirits lifted. "I am aware that I have to whip the donkey harder than I used to, but I can still make it go."

With his strong Jeffersonian theory—that government is best which governs least—with his inherited convictions on States' Rights, with his innate independence, he could not agree with all the policies of the New Deal. He thought that it weakened the nation by making the people depend on government instead of on themselves. Nevertheless, his inability to go along with his own party hurt him. He was like a lapsed Roman Catholic who cannot accept any other church.

"I tell you, Julia (the phrase was an unconscious echo of his father) the country is never going to look the same again. I did not leave the Democratic party. It left me."

In this dilemma he ceased to discuss theories of government as he had ceased to discuss religious beliefs. When pressed on the latter, he quoted Disraeli.

"What are your religious beliefs?"

"The same as those of any sensible man."

"And what is that?"

"No sensible man ever tells."

Yet after his death I found in his desk a Westminster Shorter Catechism—that plague of our childhood—in which he had crossed out the answers he doubted and left those with which he agreed. With a sensitivity equal to that of his brother-in-law Hilary Richardson about imposing his ideas on others in such important matters, he had never talked to me about it.

On his eightieth birthday one of his partners arranged to have three hundred and sixty-five friends fill the pages of a calendar book for him. The entries came from all ages, all walks of life, from many countries, some as remote as China or Australia. He opened it with pleasure, glanced at it, closed it hastily.

"I'm not going to look at this with anybody watching me."

He took it to bed with him and finished it at two o'clock. "I cried some," he said.

On this same birthday his partners gave him a dinner with speeches which all but unmanned him. The Standard Oil Company of New Jersey, not a group of sentimentalists, inscribed a silver platter, "To John W. Davis, who in a quarter of a century's association has been a living example of the law's precepts, which are: to live honorably, to injure no other man, and to render each man his due." Queen Elizabeth II appointed him a Knight of the Order of the British Empire, the highest honor she could give a foreigner. The State of South Carolina presented him with a silver tea service.

In every generation some men gain success and admiration, but for the successful and admired also to be loved is rare.

The following year, asked what he wanted for his eighty-first birthday, he had only one request to make.

"Let it pass in a decent silence."

"Growing older," he told me, "is like that old Russian story of the family crossing the steppes in a troika, pursued by wolves. They throw out first one thing and then another. Finally they throw out the baby. But still the wolves come on."

He clung to his salmon fishing as if it were the baby. Not until his last summer, when it was patently dangerous for him to climb in and out of a canoe, did his doctor persuade him to abandon it. Happily he was spared the ultimate sacrifice of giving up his work. On his mantel stood a figure of a draft horse pulling a heavy load. "I've been like that animal all my life—straining the last trace chain." His only concession to retirement was to insist that his partners cut down his share of the income from the firm. A week before his final illness several officials of a large company flew from Boston to South Carolina to get his advice.

Happily too, he did not long have to endure what he called "the multiple indignities of a hospital." He went in unconscious, and woke next morning to find his bed surrounded by white-robed nuns. His eyes wandered past them in surprise to a large picture of the bleeding heart of Jesus. Then he saw me and gave a little nod.

"So there you are," his expression said, "and I am still on earth and not in some improbable way-station."

From the beginning he saw what lay ahead and faced it with stoic calm. His senior partner came down from New York and parted from him in tears. His New York doctor gave up three days of practice to be with him. His doctors in South Carolina slept at the hospital on occasion.

With me he did not talk of the inevitable.

"You have been a good daughter to me," he said one day.

"It is easy to be good when you love," I answered.

That was all we had to say to one another, but it was enough.

Prologue for the Future

It is with regret that I leave them all, the long and loved procession, after so many hours and days spent in their company; yet it is not really a parting, for they never leave me. Because of them, because of what they were, of what their lives showed forth, my tapestry of memories has many colors. Into it has been woven the dark thread of sorrow that no human can escape, but it is mingled with the blue of joy, the crimson of courage, and everywhere the golden thread of love.

My forebears shall have neither praise nor blame for what I have become, for every one of them considered each human soul responsible for itself, uniquely and solely charged with being its own recording angel. Still, they have left me with a debt which I must pay, not to them, but to life.

They filled my growing years with so much love that I can never restore to the world the sum of it. For this I know: of all on earth which man receives or gives, earns or expends, apprehends or strives for, love is the most a loan.